PAINTING ○ COLOUR ○ HISTORY

COLLECTION PLANNED AND DIRECTED BY
ALBERT SKIRA

*A handsome book is not the work
of a single person, but a product of
the collective, well-directed efforts
of all who have contributed to its
success.*

ITALIAN PAINTING

THE CREATORS OF THE RENAISSANCE

CRITICAL STUDIES BY
LIONELLO VENTURI

HISTORICAL SURVEYS BY
ROSABIANCA SKIRA-VENTURI

TRANSLATED BY STUART GILBERT

ALBERT SKIRA

GENEVA - PARIS

THE MAKING OF THIS BOOK SYNCHRONIZED with the celebration of the Holy Year in Italy, and the fact that churches and art museums were thronged with pilgrims and visitors throughout the year might well have hampered the work of our photographic experts and engravers: a work necessitating both meticulous attention and the most delicate precision. But these difficulties were successfully overcome in every case. This success is largely due to the generous assistance we received on every hand, and it is a pleasure to record our most grateful thanks to the Minister of Fine Arts in Italy, to Curators and Directors of Museums, to private collectors and the ecclesiastical authorities, and to Dr Battisti who has given invaluable help in the ascertaining and verification of essential facts. Indeed it is thanks to the enlightened understanding and unfailing good will of all those mentioned above that we have been able to bring to a successful conclusion an enterprise which without their aid might well have proved impracticable.

CONTENTS

THE CRITICAL STUDIES * (IN ITALICS IN THE TEXT) ARE BY LIONELLO VENTURI;
THE HISTORICAL SURVEYS BY ROSABIANCA SKIRA-VENTURI.

LIST OF ILLUSTRATIONS

THE CREATORS

OF THE

RENAISSANCE

What was the Renaissance? Up to the end of the XIXth century the answer given usually took the form of a description of the characteristics whereby this period differed both from the Middle Ages and the Modern Age that followed it. But for the last forty years or more the tendency has been to look, not for the differences, but for the features in common between the close of the Middle Ages and the beginnings of the Renaissance. Those who regard the latter as an isolated phenomenon have stressed the pagan side of Humanism, whereas more recent historians have brought into prominence the religious forces which played a very considerable part in promoting that liberation of the human outlook on the world which we associate with the Renaissance. And evidently the illustrations in this volume bear out the latter view.

Indeed convincing arguments have recently been put forward to show that the notion of a Renaissance (i.e. a rebirth of man) answers to a religious aspiration prevailing throughout Christendom in the Middle Ages: a desire for a return to the origins of Christianity—which was St Francis' dream. Nor is there any doubt that the renewal of Italian culture began in the XIIIth century as a religious and moral movement, before taking a literary, artistic, philosophical and scientific turn in the XIVth and XVth centuries. Ruskin was the first to realize that the power of the Italian artists in these two centuries derived, in the last analysis, from this source of inspiration, which the Middle Ages had bequeathed to them, even though they reinforced it with an ever-widening knowledge of men and nature. True, these artists thought they were engaged in a revolution and reviving an art that had lain buried for many centuries; still it is but natural that creators of a new culture should suppose they are breaking with the immediate past, nor need we wonder if, from the XIVth century on, the Italians saw themselves as the sole representatives of civilization and light-heartedly stigmatized the age preceding theirs as "barbarian."

And, in fact, all Europe took them at their word and shared their scorn of the "Dark Ages." Until the XIXth century gave a new bias to history, the general view was that after the night of the Middle Ages, the Renaissance restored the light *of civilization to the world.   We need only recall Voltaire's opinion that in Italian art we see the first token of man's resumption of civilized life after the downfall of the Roman Empire.*

Indeed it is obvious that, gifted with vast powers of imagination, the Italians of the early Renaissance made discoveries which are still of vital import to our modern culture.   So enthusiastically did they "discover" Man that they built up a whole cult around him, extolling his dignity, his might, and his prerogatives as centre of the universe.   Not that they forgot God; they merely gave Man quasi-divine status.   It may well be that at no other moment of history was belief in Man more absolute. Yet a Space in which to locate him had to be postulated, and this Space was obviously Nature.   But here a difficulty arose; the Italians saw that, when we seek to establish a just balance between Man and Nature, the former can no longer be regarded as lord of the universe; for Nature overrules him.   But even so God held his ground; He was dispersed in the natural world, and became an all-pervading presence—though the philosophers did not as yet define this pantheism in good set terms.

For the discovery of man, as for that of nature, the legacy of classical antiquity had its importance, and indeed it once was thought to have been the real origin of the Renaissance.   To-day we know that the historical and philological research-work of the humanists was an outcome of the Renaissance, not its cause.   In other words, the ethical and religious renewal modelled on Christian antiquity advanced so far that it came to understand the creative spirit inspiring pagan antiquity as well.   Dante hailed Virgil as his master, though it was assuredly far more to St Francis that his humanism owed its origin.   In any case, our immediate concern here is with painting, and unlike the architects and sculptors, the painters of the XIVth and XVth centuries had no antique works of art available which could serve them as their models.

The rivalry between the ancients and the moderns began in the XIVth century, and, to start with, the moderns were in the ascendant.   Not until the XVIIth century were the scales tipped in favour of the ancients.

In their ways of thought and the creative processes of their artists we see much difference between the Middle Ages and the Renaissance, and an affinity between the latter and classical Antiquity.   Thus in Greece, as is common knowledge, after the archaic phase, the artists, having begun by studying nature, proceeded to idealize it, thus giving the natural object a "style."   In other words the progress of creation in their case proceeded from the concrete entity of the natural object to the abstract entity of a style.

During the Middle Ages, on the contrary, nature was disregarded; God's house was decorated with bright and varied hues so that believers might feast their eyes on a vision of heaven, and likewise of the Madonna and saints whom the painter had never seen.   Thus the artist's starting-off point was an abstract model, supplied to him by tradition, and this, in order to become a work of art, had to be transformed into a concrete portrayal inspired by mystical emotions he personally experienced.   Thus with him the creative process followed a course exactly the opposite of that followed by the classical artist; starting from an abstract content furnished by his imagination operating on a transcendental plane, he had to proceed to the concrete realization of a living figure.

During the XIIIth and XIVth centuries the Italians kept to this creative progression from the abstract to the concrete, which had been that of the Middle Ages. For all the compelling sense of reality he imparted to his art, we find this even in Giotto. But, from Masaccio onwards, the painter obviously starts out from an observation of nature in terms of structure and perspective (from concrete reality in other words), and only then allows his creative imagination to take its flight into the loftiest realm of abstraction.   The scientific analysis of optical experience which began in Florence in the first part of the XVth century influenced the whole aspect of painting for many centuries—until round about 1900, to be precise, at which time we see signs of a revival of abstract art.

This procedure instituted by the Florentines at the beginning of the XVth century came to be regarded by most connoisseurs of art as an article of aesthetic faith, and indeed has remained so.   Hence it is that all movements until quite recently—Baroque, neo-classical, romantic and realistic alike—have been based on an objective study of reality and, when reform seemed called for, always harked back to reality.   But beginning from the early years of our century, a need has been felt to reinstate the abstract as a source of inspiration—whether abstract forms and geometrical space, or the unknown, the unseen, the super-real.   Is this the revival of an age-old craving for God, or, rather, the Irrational knocking at the door of our hearts?   Anyhow, one thing is certain: that to-day we can both understand the methods of the Middle Ages, and appreciate alike two contradictory procedures—that of the XIVth-century artists who brought God down to earth and that of the XVth-century painters who raised Man up to God.   By both methods they attained perfection in the field of art, and this testimony to human grandeur which we owe to them was an exemplar for the generations that succeeded them.   And will be for generations yet unborn.

THE ART OF THE
THIRTEENTH CENTURY

Of all the arts of the West painting was the last to break free from the Byzantine style. The sculptors and architects had abandoned it as early as the XIIth century and created the Romanesque and Gothic styles, whereas even in the XIIIth century painters had not yet thought of striking out in a new direction.

Despite an opinion very prevalent in the past and endorsed even to-day by a dwindling minority, Byzantine art did not lack greatness; it sponsored an abstract phase of art in an extremely brilliant manner, the most brilliant indeed since the geometrical style of the ancient Greeks.

In delineating beings he had never seen, God and the Saints, the Byzantine artist worked by rule, keeping to symbolic formulas enjoined on him by authority and justified by tradition only. Nevertheless he was free to choose his colours, and thus it was colour, to begin with, that took effect on traditional form and, while ostensibly respecting it, brought into being a new form whose vitality was due not to contour-lines but to contrasts of colours. This new form derived from an infinite space in which light had no shade to counterbalance it: that immanent, all-pervading sheen of heaven which the painters expressed by their gold backgrounds. Moreover, it was immaterial and, lest this spiritual, mentally conceived entity should be sullied by the presence of the corporal, eschewed the third dimension. All action was ruled out; only contemplation was allowed. Thus the figure gradually dwindled down into the symbol; and we have here, in fact, iconoclasm.

The West never practised iconoclasm; nevertheless it was influenced by these schematic figures estranged from the world, which, to symbolize divinity, took on the look of phantoms. XIIIth-century Italian painting, when not of a definitely "popular" order, was, to all intents and purposes, a province of Byzantine art.

None the less, it has some outstanding figures to its credit, and one of the first is Bonaventura Berlinghieri. His "St Francis," though dated 1235 (thus only nine years after the Saint's death) is not a portrait. In this picture we do not see that best-beloved of Saints, Francis of Assisi, as he was in life; nor are we shown *anything of his noble effort to bring home to men Christ's message as something very near and vital to them, and applicable to the conduct of their everyday lives. Berlinghieri may have seen St Francis here on earth, but when he paints him, he transforms the Saint into a dweller on a transcendental plane. For on the factual plane of "real life" all is relative, and Berlinghieri's eyes are fixed on the absolute; only the infinite concerns him, not the finite. Thus the value of his art lies in its lucid evocation of that "other world" transcending ours. Immobility, two-dimensional visualization, dissociation of the elements of the thing seen—idiosyncrasies that in a Renaissance artist would be flagrant defects, here become qualities, the very "raison d'être" of the masterpiece. Into Berlinghieri's art God enters, and man is not yet admitted; and never again was a vision of transcendence to be realized with such purity of heart, nor any better capable than this of mirroring the ecstasy of the believer.*

The tales of the Saint's life and miracles flanking the portrait show a like disregard for the representation of concrete reality. A house is t h e house, a mountain is t h e mountain, a tree t h e tree, and a gesture made by the Saint t h e gesture. In short, this painting has the objectivity of "Nominalism." The Christian does not as yet participate in the lives of the beings on that higher plane; his duty is but to see, to apprehend and to adore. From the standpoint of art, however, the justification of these scenes is the life infused into the abstract forms (as in the delightful rendering of the mountain).

Besides Berlinghieri, other artists of much merit emerged during the XIIIth century, and we find wide divergences of taste amongst them. Some, like the Master of Saint Matthew, are interested chiefly in the arabesque of the composition, that is to say the decorative value of their work. For them even the most tragic events of sacred history are pretexts for plainsongs of the Gregorian type, grave and solemn, charged with restrained emotion. Others (such as the anonymous maker of the "Descent from the Cross") take amazing liberties with their line, distorting it so as to step-up the dramatic intensity of their expression. But here, the strange contortion—like a flexed willow-branch—of Christ's dead body is not merely an "Expressionist" accent; it binds together the whole composition.

In the second half of the century the Tuscan artists became alive to the fact that contrasts of light and shade produced graphic effects of a striking order; needless to say, they did not employ these for purposes of representation, since they were still guided by that abstract inspiration whose source was the supramundane. All the same their pictures now developed a complexity, a vivacity and even moral implications on the human plane that had been lacking hitherto—in fact a closer contact with reality. True, God had not yet come down to earth, but human elements were creeping into their art.

Cimabue was the Master who achieved this, for the time, amazing progress. If we compare a Cimabue "Madonna" with the work of his predecessor, the Master of the Magdalen, or with that of his contemporary, Margaritone, we realize at once that only a great genius could have reached such imaginative heights. The prominence given the throne enables him not only to uplift the divine form in space—a space which, if undefined, is certainly above the clouds upon which floats, shadowless, the light of heaven—but also to have her borne in glory by a double rank of angels; thus giving the throne the radiant majesty of some celestial palace.   This supernal vision is commented on, so to speak, upon the earth-plane by the prophets Cimabue has placed below the throne, small agitated figures who would be almost pitiful but for the grandiose setting and the superb aloofness of the divine participants.

The artist's visual conception is characterized by his contrasts of light and shade. He does not use nuances of chiaroscuro to give an illusion of solid form but, on the contrary, for contrasts of a purely pictorial effect, and to these he imparts throughout the same rhythm—alike in the throne, the wings, the aureoles, and even in the folds of the drapery, which he symbolizes by streaks of gold upon the blues and reds.

His colour harmony takes no account of light and shade; each tone stands out with a vivid intensity, so that the whole acquires the plenitude of a musical composition scored for many voices.   Indeed we have here a vast choral symphony, without a soloist, of forms, colours, images.   Hence the dignity and the sublime quality of this composition, worthy of the God it hallows; but hence, too, its limitations—the lack of individuality in its personages.

We find the same quality and the same limitations in the "Crucifixion."   The head is a dead man's, yet it retains the imprint of sufferings of the body no less than of the soul; it is a portrayal of the absolute, for all that is relative is ruled out: of the symbol without representation: of God's presence without man's presence.

But when Cimabue paints St Francis he re-emerges in the world of men.   The painter had never met the Saint; yet he painted him at Assisi, where everything, the very soil and streets, told of his presence.   Everybody knew that he was short and puny, ravaged by his self-imposed privations.   And Cimabue distorted the features of his face so as to bring out the inner tensions, the undying fire that burnt in that devoted heart.   And here those colours bright or dark, whose contrasts in the "Madonna" played upon the surface, have seeped into the flesh, testifying to the hidden life within. This glorious picture, so luminous and rich in human intimations, is unique amongst the works of Cimabue; indeed, looking ahead of the Renaissance, it heralds our modern sensibility.   Such a revelation of the inner life of the soul would have been impracticable but for the grandeur, the sublimity of Cimabue's "abstract" inspiration and his awareness of the Other World.

Pietro Cavallini, too, was a great painter; less spiritual than Cimabue, but endowed with a surer knowledge of traditional technique and more mastery of plastic form—more classical, more level-headed, so to speak.   It was his work as a mosaicist that Ghiberti most admired.   Indeed his fresco work has much of the mosaic in it; though full of a vitality due to the vivid colours and boldly stated forms, his art is objective, devoid of passion.   In respect of plastic dynamism he foreshadows Giotto.

Much more is known of Duccio di Buoninsegna, the Sienese artist who in 1285 painted the Rucellai "Madonna" for S. Maria Novella at Florence and, between 1308 and 1311 the "Maestà" in the Siena Cathedral.   Thus we can trace his evolution as an artist during twenty-five years, from his earliest to his last work.   We know something of his life, too: a rather stormy one, it seems, for he was up in arms against authority.   Making money easily, he promptly squandered it, and he died head-over-ears in debt.   But his works give no hint of the disorders of his life, the artist and the man are quite distinct.   An innovator, but a cautious, well-advised one, he delighted his fellow-citizens with his art as much as he shocked them by his conduct.

Duccio was a pupil of Cimabue, and in the Rucellai "Madonna" we find many traces of his master's style.   But alongside these are very different tendencies characteristic of Duccio's later work.   Above all he has a feeling for beauty of form that Cimabue lacked.   For Cimabue's eyes were ever fixed on the heights, on the absolute, and his conceptions were too grandiose, his moral sense was too strong, for him to pay much heed to beauty or gracefulness of line.

But, in Duccio's art, that beauty which Cimabue disdained patterns the surface of the picture, in a rhythm at once solemn and fluent which, though it lacks the vibrant intensity Cimabue imparted to his line, is subtler, more exquisitely modulated, more pleasing to the eye, and as a purely decorative value comes much nearer perfection. In his composition only the surface counts; the throne loses its importance, the attitudes of the angels are full of beauty, but we do not feel that they are uplifting the Madonna.

As regards Byzantine art and its expressionist tradition, Cimabue, though he knew no other culture, took a very personal stand.   But Duccio conforms docilely to the Byzantine decorative tradition, while adding to it some Gothic elements, notably refinement of line and, above all, an extreme elegance.

We see this, or anyhow have glimpses of it, in the Rucellai "Madonna," but it is in the "Maestà" that Duccio's style comes most conspicuously into its own.   An unfailing sense of beauty, a precise handling of the line and the gradations of the chiaroscuro, a happy ease of execution, and the charm of a soul at peace with the world—such are the constituents of Duccio's perfection.   An angel is a celestial envoy; a woman saint, the vehicle of a heavenly message.   He creates a beauty parallel to that of Greece, with, in addition, that spiritual grace which the gospels had imparted to the Christian soul.

The "Maestà," the homage paid by the saints and angels to the Madonna and Child enthroned, figures in the central panel of the front of the altarpiece.   In the predella the narrative of Christ and the Madonna begins with the Annunciation and is continued along the back, then above the "Maestà," and ends with the entombment of the Virgin.   The whole is crowned with Gothic finials.

The time factor assumes a particular importance in this sequence.   Obviously the artist's task was something more than merely depicting the sacred narrative in due order, as on a scroll—which would have but an illustrative interest.   He aimed at finding a formal rhythm which used Time for the enrichment of Space, imparting to it an undertone of mystery.   When we look at his "Christ in the Garden of Olives" we see how the twofold scene of Christ in prayer conjures up subtle mirage-like effects; Space is not rendered as a material fact, but "suggested" by successive, independent glimpses.   Thus, too, when we are shown Christ and the two apostles about to enter Emmaus, the spatial relation between the wayfarers and the gate of the town is purely psychological; the town seems located in a Space whose infinite recession is broken only by what seems the figment of a dream.

Duccio is never dramatic; even in the "Crucifixion" he is elegiac.   Thus in "The Three Marys at the Tomb" all action is arrested by the apparition of the white angel; comely, composed, master of his gestures.   The wonder and the awe which have stricken the three women into immobility is emphasized by its threefold repetition, while the mountains in the background add sublimity to the scene.

Aware that delicacy of tone can be as telling as intensity, Duccio does not indulge in hues of gem-like brilliancy; more varied, more melodious than those of his predecessors, his colours give his forms a delightful naturalness and an intimate charm. His art never attains the sublime heights scaled by Cimabue; but it is younger, freshened by the brisk north wind of Gothic.   True, in his quest of beauty he implies that the earth is aspiring heavenwards, man is yearning to share in visions of the divine.   But not man as an individual; he is a member of the Christian communion, one of a choir of voices hymning their Maker.   Perhaps, indeed, the peculiar quality of Duccio's art is this awareness that it is in the bosom of the Church alone that man draws near to God.   The Christian mystery is still a source of inspiration, but the smouldering unease, the passion has gone out of it; it has become a serene liturgical ceremony, the loveliest and noblest of religious rites.

MASTER OF SAINT MATTHEW.   CRUCIFIX (CA. 1220).   MUSEO CIVICO, PISA.   ORIGINALLY IN THE MONASTERY
OF ST MATTHEW, PISA.

THE DUECENTO

Since the beginning of the twentieth century our outlook on art has greatly broadened. In the Romantic period Late Gothic was styled "mediaeval," Stendhal must have had Raphael or Correggio at the back of his mind when he deigned to take account of Cimabue and Giotto, and English writers at the close of the nineteenth century spoke of Botticelli as a "Primitive." To-day these views strike us as narrow, to say the least of it. It would seem that, following the enthusiasm shown by painters in the early years of the present century for African art (to cite but one instance among many), we have come to think that, in the last analysis, there is no such thing as a truly "primitive" or "barbarian" art. Also we have learnt that in any given art form the choice of the methods of expression is always bound up with the artists' way of viewing the world; technical knowledge and expert execution are no longer regarded as the supreme tests of merit. In Italy, during the XVth century, artists gave much attention to problems of perspective, and closely studied the anatomy of the human body; yet it does not follow that because the artists before them took another view of the functions of representative art they should be regarded as in any way inferior.

Hence our ability to appreciate and admire, for instance, the *Crucifix* from the Monastery of St Matthew (its date is about 1220) without feeling called on to assume that the hieratic posture of Christ's body is due to any incompetence on the artist's part. Far otherwise, the special type of sensibility we find in artists of that period seems very near to us to-day, because we have come to realize it was in that period our own culture took its rise.

The painting of the late XIIIth and the XIVth century in Italy reflects the growing alteration in men's outlook on the world around them. With the reading of the Bible, and the feeling that each Christian re-lived within himself the life of the Son of God, a great, indeed a revolutionary change was coming over the world of Christendom, and this it was that led the artists towards new forms of expression, tending, as is still the case with art to-day despite the upheavals of the intervening centuries, at once to synthesize and to surpass the human situation. But this change of outlook on both the moral and the religious planes took place only gradually; moreover painting tended to lag behind sculpture and architecture, and kept much longer the imprint of Byzantine art.

That term "Byzantine art" covers a complex of tendencies which prevailed in Europe from the VIth to the XIIIth centuries and its origins are still something of a puzzle to the art-historian. What, for instance, was the part played by Byzantium itself, and what share had Antioch in Syria or Alexandria in Egypt in originating it? And, subsequently, how far was it affected by influences deriving from the outlying Byzantine provinces? All these are problems whose solution is far from easy. One thing, however, is certain : that for many centuries the same or similar forms of art were prevalent throughout the length and breadth of civilized Europe.

Byzantine art found a particularly receptive field in Italy, and many famous mosaics bear witness to its splendid flowering in the West—at Rome and Ravenna from the VIth to the IXth century, at Venice and in Sicily from the XIth to the XIIIth century. During the XIth century it was given a new direction—almost we might speak of a "Renaissance"— by the revival of certain Hellenistic traditions, one result of which was that an intensely emotional expression of the Passion of Christ was now imparted to the frescos. This new phase has been described as the "Macedonian" period, in recognition of its provincial origins, and also "Neo-Hellenic" by reason of its leanings towards realism and interest in landscape.

In Italy, alongside the distinctively Byzantine elements, we find some which are indigenous, springing so to speak spontaneously from the Italian soil; and others due to Carlovingian, Othonian or Romanesque traditions. However, in practice, it is all but impossible to sort out all these diverse trends in XIIIth-century Italian painting. On the whole we do best to regard the painting of the Duecento as the manifestation of a "province" of Byzantine art, reinforced by local contributions which gather strength with the years and little by little find fruition in the work of some original and outstanding artists whom we can definitely describe as " Italian. "

On the technical side, the graphic art of the Middle Ages found expression in mosaics, in illuminations, in fresco painting on walls and tempera painting on wood. None of these processes was new, indeed all had been employed before the Christian era ; but in this period they acquired new aspects and a wider range.

The term "mosaic" is said to come from a Greek word meaning "painstaking work, worthy of the Muses." Though uncertain, this derivation is appropriate to the patient, meticulous labours of the mosaic-worker. A mosaic consists of *tesserae*, little cubes of stone or coloured glass cemented or set in mastic on a wall. During the High Middle Ages this was the favourite medium of the Byzantines; the glowing colours of the materials employed, which shone out even in a dim light, gave them exactly what they needed to realize their ideal of an art strongly tending to the abstract.

Despite their different chromatic values, the techniques of the mosaicist and the fresco-painter were very similar. Indeed, quite often a preliminary lay-out in fresco served the former as the basis for his decoration in mosaic. It should, however, be noted that when the workers in mosaic tried to adapt their technique to effects more suited to the fresco, their work lost its originality and fell short of the high artistic standard they attained when they kept in view the requirements of their own *métier*.

Until the invention of the printing-press in the XVth century, artists found in the miniatures figuring in illuminated manuscripts a congenial form of expression. The word "miniature" derives from "minium" (red oxide of lead), the colour employed for the ornamental head-letters *(lettrines)* at the beginning of each page in ancient manuscripts. Since a book could easily be carried from place to place, these illuminations greatly furthered the exchange of ideas on art, and this art flourished in many widely separated countries.

The fresco-process was the technique that lasted longest—flourishing, indeed, until quite late in our era—and it developed prodigiously during the Middle Ages and the Renaissance. The pigments were applied direct or mixed with water on to a surface composed of mixed lime and sand. Lime when mixed with sand and water forms a coat of wet plaster into which the colour can sink, solidifying as it dries. For good results the plaster must dry slowly and some powdered marble was often added, as this was found to ameliorate the process. A special difficulty of fresco-painting is that the painter has to put on his colours rapidly, before the plaster has time to dry, and to dispense with retouching. Also he must bear in mind that the colours will have changed considerably, when dry. Another handicap is that certain colours, such as lake and bronze-green, must be ruled out, because the chemical constituents of the lime affect them injuriously.

The origins of the fresco go back to the dawn of history, indeed beyond it, to the night of the prehistoric. It was widely employed in all the civilizations we know, and is often hard to distinguish from tempera painting, whose technique is similar.

For painting on wood or a surface other than a wall, the typically Italian method (which persisted until painting in oils came in) was that in which tempera is used, the binding material mixed with the powdered pigment being as a rule the white of egg. In tempera painting the panels were first given a coat of plaster of Paris mixed with glue ; sometimes, too, a covering of linen, leather or parchment was stretched on them. And even earlier than the XIVth century the practice came in of giving the panels a coat of varnish once the paint had dried.

Quite a number of early accounts of the various art techniques of the Middle Ages and Renaissance are extant. Thus Cennino Cennini in his *Libro dell'Arte* has much to tell us of painting in the XIVth century, while for the next century we have the treatise of L. B. Alberti (1404-1472), and these books may rank as the best introduction to the art of the Renaissance and its aspirations. And, finally, at the end of the same century, Leonardo da Vinci began his *Treatise of Painting*, which renders the same service to the pictorial art of the XVIth century.

MASTER OF SAINT MATTHEW.   WOMEN WEEPING OVER THE BODY OF CHRIST.   FRAGMENT OF THE CRUCIFIX (CA. 1220).
MUSEO CIVICO, PISA.   ORIGINALLY IN THE MONASTERY OF ST MATTHEW, PISA.

The first to give an historical account of the Florentine, Sienese and Roman painters was Lorenzo Ghiberti (1378-1455), who made the " Golden Gates " of the Baptistery of Florence. In his *Commentarii* (written in the middle of the XVth century), he deals with the painters from the XIIIth up to approximately the mid-XIVth century, making it clear that, in his opinion, their art was superior to that of his own times. (We may mention that all the information he provides is scrupulously accurate.)

Other sources are the writings of the humanist men of letters, but most important of all is the fact that, beginning in the first half of the XVIth century, complete records were compiled at Florence, as well as at Venice and Naples, of all the facts that could be ascertained regarding the lives of the painters. These were the materials drawn on by Giorgio Vasari (1511-1574) for his *Lives of the Most Eminent Painters, Sculptors and Architects*, published first in 1550 and reissued in 1568, which was and remains the necessary source-book for all students of Renaissance art.

Vasari was a Mannerist painter, a follower of Michelangelo, and he viewed the course of art from the XIIIth century up to his day as a steady progress culminating in the supreme perfection of Michelangelo. He has more to tell us of the human side of the artists' lives than of their creative activity, often indulges in rather trivial anecdotes, and retails dubious legends, even inventing some himself. But it should be added that his intuitions were far happier than his views on art and the way its history should be written, and that, despite inaccuracies and romancings, his great work is a not unworthy mirror of the glories of the Renaissance.

The XIIIth-century works we shall describe all hail from Tuscany. During this period, their family likeness was so great that not only may Tuscany be regarded as a province of that far-flung art whose nominal metropolis was Byzantium, but the ascription of paintings of this time to their respective artists has been no easy matter—especially in view of the scantiness of the written information regarding them that has come down to us. Attempts have been made to distinguish the schools of art centering in famous cities : the Schools of Lucca, Pisa, Siena, Florence. But, in reality, these centres had not yet developed sufficiently well-defined local " personalities " for us to be able to speak authoritatively of one school or another. Not until the XIVth century did the Florentine and Sienese schools strike out on their own distinctive lines.

Vasari shared in the traditional view that the painting previous to Giotto was essentially " Greek " (by which he meant Byzantine) and that Giotto brought about a revolution in painting by giving it a definitely Latin form. True, we find in Tuscan works of art during the XIIth and XIIIth centuries the stiffness and the leaning towards an abstract rendering of forms and attitudes which characterize Byzantine art. Yet already we can see different tendencies at work within them.

Thus the *Crucifix* now in the Pisa Museum may be held to illustrate a tendency towards decorative art. It was originally in St Matthew's Monastery, its maker is unknown, but we can fix its date approximately as 1220. Here the figure of Christ forms a whole with the numerous background scenes illustrating incidents of his life. The clean-cut structure of the cross and the emphasis laid on the decorative elements give this work an elegance rarely attained before. Christ's eyes are closed in death, his head is drooping helplessly, forlornly, upon his shoulder, whose undulating line smoothly carries on the movement of the arms. This rhythm pervading the body as a whole brings out the fluent grace of the linework. Here the appeal is less to our adoration than to our love ; this is not the Christ triumphant, open-eyed, shown us in most pictures of the period, and its poignantly human emotion ranks this as one of the most poetic works of XIIIth-century Italian art.

The scenes in the background read from top to bottom. Beginning on the left, we see the Descent from the Cross, the mourning over Christ's body, the laying in the tomb, and the Marys at the sepulchre. The last-but-one panel has two simultaneous scenes : the journey to, and the supper at, Emmaus. The final panel shows Christ appearing to the apostles. In the scene of the mourning over Christ's body, Christ lies outstretched on the knees of the Virgin and St Joseph of Arimathaea. With all the very human tenderness and grief that it expresses, the rhythm of the hands, the aureoles and the heads has an elegiac cadence and a value essentially decorative. The lay-out of the figures is paralleled by the line formed by the angels. Their wings outspread against a golden sky, they bear aloft the shroud, forming a curve converging on the point of strongest emotional interest and emphasizing the poetic quality of the forms of Christ and his Mother. This scene, so often and so diversely portrayed in art, does not here convey a sense of tragedy ; rather, it is a gentle dirge in which, with quiet harmonies of line and colour, grief is transmuted into poetry.

The picture of St Francis was made some years later than the *Crucifix* of St Matthew's Monastery. It is signed Bonaventura Berlinghieri and dated 1235. We know something about the artist's father, who made his name at the beginning of the XIIIth century and, coming from Milan, introduced Lombard art traditions into Tuscany. He had three sons, all of whom were painters, but the work of one only, Bonaventura, is known to us. He is mentioned in records of the City of Lucca in 1228 for the first time, and after that at various dates up to 1274. Only one of this painter's works is extant : the *St Francis* of the church at Pescia, probably an early work ; indeed the death of St Francis had taken place only a few years before the date inscribed on the panel.

The part played by St Francis in the development of Christianity was a great and noble one. Born at Assisi in September 1181 or 1182, of a family of well-to-do linen-merchants, he brought about by his writings, his teachings, and the example of his life, round which so many legends clustered, a change of heart throughout the Christian world. He combined the most active mysticism with an asceticism hostile to every form of self-indulgence. But what, most of all, has fired the world's imagination is "love for all things great and small," his gratitude to the Creator for the manifold beauties of nature, and the infinite gentleness and kindliness of his outlook on life. No less than in the *Fioretti*, we find in his *Cantico di Frate Sole* (written about 1225) that almost childlike simplicity, that humble yet joyous adoration of his Maker, to which is due the worldwide influence of this great mystic and his message. For him, those words "God the Father" carried their fullest meaning : God was at once the father of that divine Child whose very name thrilled with reverent joy all who visited the "Christ-child's Crib" built by the Saint in the woodlands near Assisi, and, likewise, the loving Father of all men. St Francis made the teachings of Christ a living reality here on earth, and brought home to men their moral value, without troubling overmuch about their theological implications. And it was for this reason—because it appealed directly to the heart, humbly adapting itself to the human situation—that St Francis' example opened a new path to Christendom.

Bonaventura Berlinghieri was obviously impressed by the inspiring personality of this Saint, who was almost his contemporary ; but he did not see in him the man whose intimate communion with the divine had brought it very near to men, a friendly presence. What gripped him was, rather, the divinity immanent in that saintly figure. He shows us the *povero* of Assisi in his long brown robe, standing in a posture of almost startling rigidity against a gold and coloured background portraying scenes of his life and his miracles. His feet do not touch the ground and the open hand which has received the stigmata might well be warning us away. Such is the amazing power and expressiveness of this figure that we almost feel the painter sought here to portray not the man who lived, but a visitant from another world, the human element merged in the mystic. The planes are disposed in sharp angles, the lines convey only essentials, and the angularity of the features, the tonsure, even the projecting ears, combine to give the saint's gaze its curiously concentrated expression. Here the soul is everything, the body but its husk ; a transparent veil through which we glimpse the mystery of the divine.

The picture of the saint is surrounded by six scenes ; two of them illustrating episodes of his life, as against four portraying miracles. This proportion is worth noting ; some fifty years later Giotto, when treating the same theme, laid most stress on the saint's life, only

SCHOOL OF BERLINGHIERI. DESCENT FROM THE CROSS. FRAGMENT : CRUCIFIX.
UFFIZI, FLORENCE.

BONAVENTURA BERLINGHIERI. ST FRANCIS AND SCENES FROM HIS LIFE, 1235. (59 ½ × 45¾ ")
CHURCH OF S. FRANCESCO, PESCIA.

BONAVENTURA BERLINGHIERI. ST FRANCIS AND SCENES FROM HIS LIFE. FRAGMENT : ST FRANCIS RECEIVING THE STIGMATA. CHURCH OF S. FRANCESCO, PESCIA.

allotting two panels to the miracles. In fact, in these two painters, the religious sentiment took different trends, and the content of their work differed accordingly, as did their methods of execution. The two incidents in the life of St Francis depicted by Berlinghieri are : *St Francis receiving the Stigmata* and *St Francis preaching to the Birds*. In the former we clearly see the representational procedure adopted by Berlinghieri. Though the forms, bounded by lines, seem to be located in space, this is more an illusion than a reality. Each element of the picture has an independent value ; thus the artist not only accords as much importance to the mountain and the tower as to St Francis himself, but bestows the same attention on the decorative features that stress the architecture. We may see a legacy of folk art in this tendency to express reality by "abstract" lines.

BONAVENTURA BERLINGHIERI. ST FRANCIS AND SCENES FROM HIS LIFE. FRAGMENT: ST FRANCIS PREACHING
TO THE BIRDS. CHURCH OF S. FRANCESCO, PESCIA.

In the *Crucifix* of St Matthew's Monastery we have seen a decorative tendency emerging, applied to the rhythms of the line without regard to differences of plane. In Berlinghieri,
however, we find an attempt precisely to define the object represented. Other painters (who
may be grouped round Giunta Pisano) were to attempt a more dramatic portrayal by the use
of distorted lines. And, later, Cimabue was to carry to a high pitch a method centering
especially on effects of light and shade, which we may describe as "luminist"—adopting an
Italian term which seems exactly to describe this procedure, of which there were already
intimations in certain works by Coppo di Marcovaldo, amongst others.

A *Crucifix* now in the Uffizi may be said to belong to the school of Berlinghieri, though
perhaps this work shows more expressionist tendencies. In the detail here reproduced, *The
Descent from the Cross*, we may note that the elements of the composition and the individual

NE DESP
ET IS.
UOS QUI
PECCARE
SOLETIS.
EXEMPLO
OB MEO.
UOS REPA
RATE DE
O.

MASTER OF THE MAGDALEN.   THE MAGDALEN AND SCENES FROM HER LIFE.
(64 ¼ × 30″)   ACADEMY, FLORENCE.

figures are reduced to a minimum, the figures being rather symbols than portrayals. Nevertheless, we cannot but be moved by the emotional tension, the imprint of grief which marks each element.

A painter who had success in his time and was thought highly of by the early Florentine art-critics was Margaritone d'Arezzo. Vasari writes of him at length, naming several of his works and mentioning that he was also an architect. Several portraits of St Francis, bearing his signature, are extant. He obviously tried to humanize the saint, and also to break away from the "frontalism" of his predecessors by an attempt to render volumes, three-dimensional mass. But his execution was somewhat uninspired and harsh. Historically speaking, no doubt, Margaritone is nearer St Francis than was Bonaventura Berlinghieri, but his feeble portraiture and total unawareness of space betoken a backward step as regards his senior's achievement.

An outstanding work by Margaritone is his *Madonna*, now in London, on which we read the signature *Margaritus de Aritio me fecit*. Vasari admires the "grace" of this picture and says that it ranks highly not only because the scenes depicted in it are so well done that they seem like illuminations, but also and chiefly because the artist attained such *finesse* of execution, when painting on very thin linen affixed to a wooden panel. In this picture Margaritone gave free rein to his instinct for decoration, indeed it has much in common with certain textiles. On the gold background plays a glittering profusion of patches of colour made by the figures and elements of the various scenes, and this "pointillist" technique is carried on into the setting, which is dotted with tiny decorative figurines. Here the miniature-like daintiness with which the stories are narrated and the vivacity of the colours are typically Byzantine in spirit. This painter was a contemporary of Cimabue but, while the latter was first to sponsor a new trend in taste, Margaritone was merely a continuer of a tradition already venerable.

The name of the man who painted the *Magdalen* and the story of her life being unknown, he is styled "the Master of the *Magdalen*." He seems to have practised his art over two decades, from 1250 to 1270, and his habit, obviously purposive, of detaching the central figure from the scenes surrounding it affiliates him to Berlinghieri. But the Master of the *Magdalen* was far from feeling the same compulsion to give his elements an abstract quality, and his art is more popular, more decorative. Though this work lacks the dynamism of the *St Francis*, its colours are remarkably effective and this, together with the imaginative treatment of decorative forms, accounts for the charm this picture undoubtedly possesses.

MARGARITONE D'AREZZO. MADONNA AND CHILD. (33 × 69″) NATIONAL GALLERY, LONDON.

CIMABUE

" By reason of the vast flood of misfortunes that had afflicted and engulfed unhappy Italy, not only had what we may call the artists' 'workshops' fallen into ruin, but (and this surely was much graver) the whole race of artists had died out. And now it was, by the goodness of God, that there was born in Florence, in the Year of Grace 1240, one Giovanni named Cimabue, who led forth the new dawn of painting. " With these words Vasari begins his life of Cimabue, thus endorsing a tradition of long standing which set up Cimabue as the greatest painter of the whole XIIIth century. His merits as an artist had already been acclaimed by Dante and, following his lead, by all Florentine writers. Indeed even to-day he is the most popular of the painters of his age.

Nevertheless, our information regarding Cenni di Peppo, known as Cimabue, is scanty. The date of his birth as given by Vasari lacks confirmation, and the first definite mention we have of him is that in 1272 he was in Rome. Some have taken this to mean that he was working there, or even that he was educated there, but this seems unlikely. In 1301-02 we know he was at Pisa, painting a *Maestà* for the Church of Santa Chiara, and completed the mosaic of the apse of the Duomo much of the work on which had been done by a certain Francesco ; Cimabue painted the figure of St John.

The early Florentine writers on art attributed to Cimabue so many works and in such diverse styles that, at first, given the paucity of dates, art-historians were frankly bewildered and even drew the conclusion that the name "Cimabue" was merely a compendious label for various *ignoti*. Now, however, we have succeeded in sorting out a certain number of works which are unquestionably his and in which his personality is manifest.

The attribution to Cimabue of the *Crucifix* in the Church of S. Domenico at Arezzo is of comparatively recent date, but it is now endorsed by all expert opinion, as is his collaboration on the frescos at the Baptistery in Florence. The former is a work of the painter's early years. Though its affinities with other works of the period are obvious, Cimabue displays in it an emotive realism that was something new in art. A decorative background replaces the scenes which usually accompanied a *Crucifixion*, and the figure of the Crucified stands out in lonely eminence. It is to the way in which Cimabue focuses our interest on the play of light and shade which gives the body its solidity, and brings out the expressiveness of the face, that is due the strong effect made by this picture. And in the pathetic forlornness of this lonely figure with closed eyes we have a portrayal, carrying entire conviction, of a grief passing all human griefs. This exceptional sensitivity in the treatment of his themes is one of the reasons why Cimabue has always been acclaimed as one of the leaders of Italian painting.

A great number of his works figure in the Upper and Lower Churches of S. Francesco at Assisi ; the paintings in the transept and the choir of the former are his work. Unfortunately these frescos have suffered with the years and their present state is lamentable. Owing to some curious chemical process, the bright and dark colours have gradually become interchanged, with the result that what we see is a sort of " negative " of the original. Nevertheless, the compelling power of the drawing remains intact and, through the strange mutation of the colours, the spectator feels he is glimpsing a tragedy enacted in some spectral world.

In the Lower Church is a *Madonna and Child with Angels and St Francis*. In the representation of the saint, the artist's psychological insight and emotional response are so intense that we feel we are looking at a portrait. Not that it necessarily resembles the man who was St Francis—that, anyhow, is beyond our knowing—but because each element of his personality is as it were crystallized, shining forth with a gem-like clarity. This is far indeed from the wraithlike saint whom Berlinghieri showed us ; we feel that he is very near and very human, a man amongst men, but one illuminated by the mission to which he gave his life.

At the Uffizi is a *Madonna Enthroned* (originally in the Church of the Holy Trinity) in which we find a new tendency towards monumental structure, and composition on broad

CIMABUE (FL. 1272-1302). CRUCIFIX (DETAIL). CHURCH OF S. DOMENICO,
AREZZO.

tectonic lines. All mediaeval art was governed by the principle of its subordination to architecture. Thus French Gothic aimed at a co-operation of all the parts in the service of an architectural *ensemble*—which is why painting pure and simple failed to make progress in regions where the Gothic spirit was paramount. In this *Madonna Enthroned* we may note the importance ascribed by the painter to the throne, the architectural element inserted in his picture ; indeed it plays the leading part, that of carrying and encompassing the Madonna. Cimabue has used his angels to impart a circling movement, described by the ring of aureoles round the throne, which does not rest on a massive pedestal but on a group of hollow niches. Thus we are given an impression that the Madonna is actually being borne aloft " in glory " by the angels.

What gives Cimabue's art its exceptional power is its expression of the sublime—which, in a fashion, sums up all the tendencies of his predecessors. He was not influenced by that taste for the Gothic which made itself so widely felt in the sculpture and architecture of his day ; nor was he attracted by the beauty, elegance or refinement of the idealized human individual ; in its greatness—and within its limits—his art is transcendental.

CIMABUE (FL. 1272-1302). ST FRANCIS (DETAIL). FRESCO,
LOWER CHURCH OF S. FRANCESCO, ASSISI

CIMABUE (FL. 1272-1302). MADONNA ENTHRONED. (152 × 117¾")
UFFIZI, FLORENCE.

P. CAVALLINI (FL. 1273-CA.1330). CHRIST WITH THE APOSTLES (DETAIL). FRESCO,
CHURCH OF S. CECILIA, ROME.

PIETRO CAVALLINI

Time and chance have played a curious part in the renown of Cavallini. Little or nothing is said about him in the records that have come down to us, and over a very long period his was an inconspicuous name in art history, since the only known works by him were his mosaics. Then, in 1899-1900, with the discovery of the frescos of S. Cecilia's Church in Rome, it at last became possible to assign this artist his due place amongst the pioneers of Italian painting at the close of the XIIIth century.

As early as the XVth century Cavallini was held in high esteem, and we may feel sure that Ghiberti was voicing the considered opinion of his age when he wrote : " There was in Rome a master of a skill that none could rival and a tireless worker ; his name was Pietro Cavallini. " And again, speaking of Cavallini's mosaics : " I make bold to say that never have I seen mosaics done so well, " and describing him as *nobilissimo*, adds that he painted "single-handed" the frescos in the Church of S. Cecilia. It is noteworthy that in his *Commentarii* Ghiberti makes mention of no other master of the Roman School.

We have no record of the date of Cavallini's birth, and not only is the chronology of his works uncertain, but it is hard to decide exactly what works are his. In or about the year 1292 he made the mosaics for the Church of S. Maria in Trastevere. In certain portions of this work we find an attempt to render space more freely, but in general Byzantine influences still are paramount. In this connexion Muratoff observes that " here we have obviously a mingling of Western and Gothic elements with methods inherited by him from the Venetian mosaic-workers in the Byzantine tradition. "

Some have thought to see the work of Cavallini and his pupils in the mural decorations of the Upper Church of S. Francesco at Assisi — above those of Giotto. These frescos, which portray the *Blessings of Isaac*, rate high as works of art ; it is, however, far from easy to decide who painted them.

We see Cavallini at his splendid best in the frescos at S. Cecilia in Rome ; here his art is more personal and less subservient to tradition. A large fragment has survived, the scene of the *Last Judgement*. Christ is the central figure, and around him are the Apostles, " haughty and stern as righteous judges, " as they have been described. Seated in high-backed chairs, in a semi-circle, they are focussing their gaze on Christ. There is something statuesque in their attitudes, which vary only slightly from figure to figure, and the impression made by this picture is one of august dignity, the majesty of a celestial conclave.

Here it is obvious that Cavallini has set himself to rendering plastic form by means of chiaroscuro. The colour is deep and velvety, rich in undertones, and lighter passages in softer colours juxtapose the darker. Though clearly the artist had studied to advantage Neo-Hellenistic forms, he definitely broke away in this fresco from the earlier Byzantine tendencies.

Cavallini's way of handling plastic form has suggestions of a certain aspect of Giotto's art— he has the same rather heavy way of rendering drapery—but it is difficult to establish any real connexion. Struck by the affinities between these artists, Vasari actually asserts (with a fine disregard of chronology) that Cavallini was Giotto's pupil, and this has added to the confusion surrounding Cavallini's career and personality.

In 1308 Charles II, King of Naples, invited Cavallini to visit his court, and he did some painting during this visit. Only some portions of the murals in the Church of S. Maria in Donna Regina seem to be by the same hand as the Santa Cecilia frescos in Rome.

The originality of Cavallini's art is apparent to-day, when we see it in its historical setting. While based to some extent, perhaps, on forms belonging to the Neo-Hellenistic tradition, it has a nobility and a simplicity ranking it beside the work of the Great Masters of XIVth-century Italy. It would be rash to assume that Cavallini was the only Roman artist of the period to feel the need for new forms ; unfortunately the information available as to the state of Roman art at this time is too meagre for us to come to any definite conclusion.

DUCCIO (?-1319). MADONNA ENTHRONED (RUCELLAI MADONNA). (177¾ × 114″)
UFFIZI, FLORENCE.

DUCCIO DI BUONINSEGNA

Younger than Cimabue, slightly older than Giotto, and a contemporary of Cavallini, Duccio di Buoninsegna, the Sienese (the exact date of his birth is uncertain), belongs to a period of transition and to that generation which, though strongly imbued with the Byzantine and mediaeval spirit, witnessed the rise of artists with leanings towards the Gothic style. Historically too, the period was transitional. On September 4, 1260, the Sienese defeated the Florentines in the battle of Montaperti and as a result of this victory the city of Siena entered on a phase of great prosperity, which found expression in the 1277 *coup d'état* when the rich merchants and burghers of the city seized the reins of power. The evolution of Sienese art was not so rapid. And Duccio always remained faithful to the tradition of the Church. It was only with the next generation that art came wholly under the sway of aristocratic forms, or the influence of the powerful middle-class.

The first recorded date concerning Duccio's activities is 1278, when a payment was made him for decorating the panels of a chest containing the appurtenances of the municipality. It must not be thought that work of this kind was regarded as "minor"; on the contrary, it ranked high throughout this period. Thus the most eminent painters of the day were called upon to decorate the "Biccherna" books—the ledgers in which the accounts of the city were recorded—and this tradition lasted on till the end of the XVth century.

Duccio had a checkered career : he was often in financial straits, of which the records give us frequent and detailed accounts. In 1280 he was sentenced to pay a fine—nothing is known of the circumstances—nor is there anything in the records to tell us if he continued living in Siena during the next five years. Quite possibly, in consequence of the sentence passed on him, he migrated to Florence, where he certainly was on April 15, 1285, the Chapter of Santa Maria Novella having commissioned him to paint a Madonna for this church. This picture has been identified by almost all art-critics as the Rucellai *Madonna* now in the Uffizi. Vasari took this to be by Cimabue, and admittedly there is much in it that obviously recalls his style ; nevertheless it also has many of the characteristics of Duccio's art. (Hence the theory that quite probably Duccio was a pupil of Cimabue.)

Though both theme and lay-out resemble those of Cimabue, the painter of the Rucellai *Madonna* has succeeded in infusing into this work a very different spiritual conception ; nor does he show the same concern for the structural lay-out of the picture. Here we have a Madonna aloof, as in Byzantine art, and the angels round her no longer form an aureole contributing to the build-up ; rather, they are an element of grace, like her throne, which has all but been transformed into a mass of drapery. Also we see a feeling for beauty, in other words for that harmonious form, rich in intimations, which is both peculiarly Gothic and one of the essential characteristics of Duccio's art.

From 1291 onwards we have fairly copious records of Duccio's life ; many details of it, trivial in themselves, have a psychological value, as throwing light on the kind of man he was. Round about 1295, when he was invited to join a committee appointed to select the site for a new fountain, Duccio was evidently quite well off ; he owned a house, bought wine, and even lent out money. True, he was fined again, but presumably there was nothing serious in his offence as the fine was small and, moreover, in 1298 we hear of him as a member of the "Radota," a sort of advisory board appointed by the Government. But it is clear that the artist had not only extravagant habits, but an impulsive, unruly disposition.

In 1299 Duccio was sentenced to pay a very heavy fine for refusing to take the oath of fidelity to the Captain of the People, and 1302 he paid two more fines, the second for insubordination. One wonders what form this "insubordination" took ; was it political or simply personal? No information is vouchsafed in the records. But these glimpses of his career reveal the curious contradiction between the painter's life and his art : the former all unruliness and independence, the latter a constant aspiration towards pure, harmonious forms, and almost wholly governed by the established tradition of religious art.

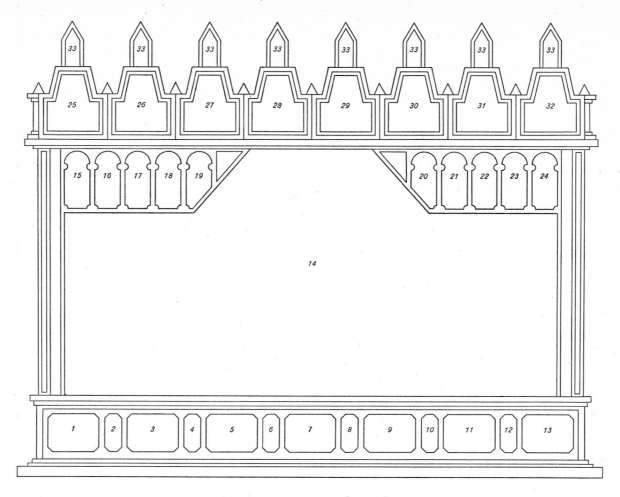

DUCCIO. PLAN OF THE MAESTA (FRONT). *(See page 41.)*

In 1308 the chapter of the Siena Cathedral commissioned him to paint a big *Madonna in Maestà* ; this has come down to us almost intact and ranks to-day as his major work. The contract, drawn up in due and proper form between Duccio and his employers, makes entertaining reading, hinting as it does pretty clearly that the latter were far from feeling entire confidence in the artist. Seemingly they doubted if he would ever bring his work to completion, for they drew up an elaborate and detailed time-table and made a point of placing all the materials needed for the work at his immediate disposal, so that the painter was required " only to supply his presence and the labour of his hands." Besides the *Madonna* we have, in the predella, a large number of scenes painted on the back and along the top, representing a great volume of work, which Duccio, erratic as he was, carried out within the specified period of three years, thus proving his employers' lack of confidence unjustified in the event.

An old chronicle tells us of the wild enthusiasm of the townsfolk of Siena when they carried this work in triumph from his studio to the Cathedral. " On the day (June 9, 1311) when the *Maestà* was brought to the Duomo, all shops were closed and the Bishop ordained that there should be a great procession in which a goodly number of priests and holy Brothers were to join, accompanied by the Nine, the notables of the Commune and the people of Siena. And sure enough all the townsfolk flocked together to the *Maestà* and, lining up, marched in good order round the Campo as the custom is. The bells rang out a festal peal to welcome in this most noble altarpiece made by Duccio di Niccolo, painter, plying his trade in the house of the Muciatti outside the walls of Stalloreggi. All the day was given over to devotions and the worshippers freely dispensed alms to the poor, beseeching God and his Mother, who is our intercessor, that, in her infinite mercy, she should protect us from all ills and pestilences, and defend us against the enemies from without and the enemies within our gates. "

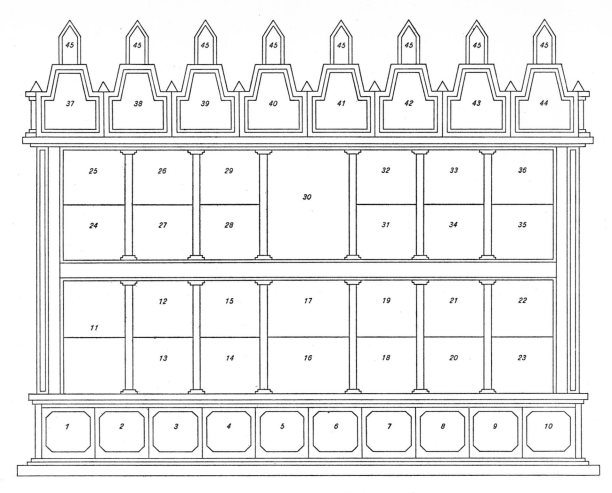

DUCCIO.   PLAN OF THE MAESTA (BACK).

Reference has been made to Duccio's famous altarpiece, the *Maestà*, painted on both sides of a panel which was subsequently sawn up into parts.   The greater part of this altarpiece is preserved in the " Opera del Duomo " at Siena.   The front shows " The Madonna in Glory " (Maestà) while the back is divided into compartments narrating the Life of Christ.

The numbers on the plan denote the following scenes :

Front :

1. Annunciation (National Gallery, London).
2. Isaiah (Berlin Museum).
3. Nativity (Berlin Museum).
4. Ezekiel (Berlin Museum).
5. Adoration of the Magi.
6. Solomon.
7. Presentation in the Temple.
8. Malachi.
9. Massacre of the Innocents.
10. Jeremiah.
11. The Flight into Egypt.
12. Hosea.
13. The Child Jesus in the Temple.
14. Maestà.
15. Thaddaeus.
16. Simon.
17. Philip.
18. James the Greater.
19. Andrew.
20. Matthew.
21. James the Less.
22. Bartholomew.
23. Thomas.
24. Matthias.
25. Annunciation of the Death of Mary.
26. Mary takes leave of John.
27. Mary takes leave of the Apostles.
28. Death of Mary.
29. Funeral Rites of Mary.
30. Entombment of Mary.
31. Assumption of the Virgin.
32. Coronation of the Virgin.
33. Angel.

Back :

1. Baptism of Christ.
2. The First Temptation.
3. The Temptation on a Pinnacle of the Temple.
4. The Temptation on the Mountain-top (Frick Collection, New York).
5. The Vocation of Peter and Andrew (Rockefeller Collection, New York).
6. The Marriage at Cana.
7. Christ and the Woman of Samaria (Rockefeller Collection, New York).
8. Christ healing the Blind (National Gallery, London).
9. The Transfiguration (National Gallery, London).
10. Raising of Lazarus (C. H. Mackay Collection, New York).
11. The Entrance into Jerusalem.
12. The Washing of Feet.
13. The Last Supper.
14. Christ taking leave of the Apostles.
15. The Covenant of Judas.
16. The Garden of Olives.
17. The Kiss of Judas.
18. St Peter's Denial.
19. Christ before Annas.
20. Christ before Caiaphas.
21. Christ buffeted.
22. The Pharisees arraigning Christ.
23. Pilate questioning Christ.
24. Christ before Herod.
25. Christ before Pilate.
26. Christ scourged.
27. The Crowning with Thorns.
28. Pilate washing his Hands.
29. Calvary.
30. The Crucifixion.
31. Descent from the Cross.
32. The Entombment.
33. The three Marys at the Tomb.
34. The Descent into Limbo.
35. Noli me tangere.
36. The Way to Emmaus.
37. Christ appearing to the Apostles.
38. The Disbelief of Thomas.
39. Christ appearing beside the Lake of Tiberias.
40. Christ talking with Peter.
41. Christ appearing to the Apostles on a Mountain in Galilee.
42. Christ appearing to the Apostles in the Upper Room.
43. The Ascension.
44. Pentecost.
45. Angel.

DUCCIO (?-1319).   MAESTA.   DETAIL FROM THE BACK : THE THREE MARYS AT THE TOMB.   OPERA DEL DUOMO, SIENA.

This was Duccio's hour of triumph.   A short-lived triumph, for only two years later he was so heavily in debt that he was forced to sell everything he owned.   When, about 1319, he died, his family had to renounce the inheritance crippled with debts and mortgages.

The plan we give of the *Maestà* shows the lay-out of the altarpiece, painted on both sides, since it was to adorn the central altar of the Cathedral and be visible from both nave and choir.   Later, it was sawn in two, lengthwise ; several scenes of the front, cut from their setting, have found their way to various museums, while some have disappeared.

On the whole, this work has stood up well to the ravages of time, and we can see it almost as it originally was, in the Cathedral Museum at Siena.   The front shows us the Madonna and Child, and the back several episodes in the lives of Christ and the Madonna.

We reproduce three of Duccio's narrative scenes, illustrating the different ways in which his imagination worked.   The scene of the *Three Marys at the Tomb* is imbued with that sense of the magical, those intimations of a world beyond our ken, which in Duccio's art replaces dramatic effect—for effects of that order would have been out of keeping with the ideal he had set himself.   The *Way to Emmaus* illustrates his conception of space, a space not so much shown as a visual entity as implied by breaks in continuity.   And, lastly, in *Christ in the Garden of Olives*, we see how Duccio manages to combine space and time, by creating a rhythm accompanying in the distance the sequence of events he is narrating.

This introduction of the concept of time into the portrayal of space is a characteristic procedure of mediaeval art ; one of the changes brought by the Renaissance was its exclusion of the concept of duration by concentrating on the here-and-now of space.

42

DUCCIO (?-1319). MAESTA. DETAIL FROM THE BACK: THE WAY TO EMMAUS. OPERA DEL DUOMO, SIENA.

DUCCIO (?-1319). MAESTA. DETAIL FROM THE BACK: THE GARDEN OF OLIVES. OPERA DEL DUOMO, SIENA.

DUCCIO (?-1319). MAESTA. DETAIL FROM THE FRONT : ANGEL. OPERA DEL DUOMO, SIENA.

GIOTTO AND MASO

Before considering Giotto from the modern angle, we may do well to glance at appraisals of his art by the men of his own age; for it is obvious that they were vastly impressed by it and that, to their mind, he changed the whole aspect and significance of painting.   While Dante merely tells us that Giotto's fame eclipsed that of Cimabue, Boccaccio puts it more strongly, declaring that he resuscitated painting after it had been "in the grave" for many centuries.   This is perhaps the first indication we have of any contemporary awareness of a Renaissance, and it is noteworthy that it was painting which gave rise to this conception.   Cennino Cennini shares this view, but puts it in a different way; Giotto, he says, translated into Latin the language of painting, which had hitherto been Greek (i. e. Byzantine). Thus clearly Cennini was alive to the fact that Italy now was breaking with the art-culture of the East and striking out in a direction of her own.   Lastly, we may note that, before the end of the XIVth century, such writers as Sacchetti and Filippo Villani agreed that Giotto was the supreme painter, and, while recognizing the talent of his pupils, denied that any had equalled him.   For the notion of "progress" in art had not yet corrupted judgement, and the individual artist's genius was held to be the sole criterion of merit.

There is no doubt that the interest of his contemporaries in Giotto's art centered on its plastic effect. Obviously, indeed, when confronted by his solidly convincing, well-defined portrayals, those of such men as Cimabue and Duccio must have seemed vague and wraithlike.   And since these plastic qualities always give a picture a material aspect—as though it could be palpably felt and measured—, Giotto's art seemed to belong to the world of terra firma more than to the world celestial.   Moreover the Florentines knew Latin well enough to have read the classical descriptions of art as being "the imitation of nature," and they accounted for the exciting impression Giotto's work produced on them as being due to some prodigious feat of craftsmanship, enabling them to see in his art, more even than imitation, the very face of nature herself.

This is Boccaccio's view; but he goes on to add that while Giotto's predecessors had charmed the eyes of the ignorant, he, Giotto, courted the intelligence of the wise. This manner of interpreting art, which was a new one, had its point; for Giotto's figures have their place in life; they love and hate, they act and sometimes dream. Whereas in Duccio's works, for instance, always the shadow of the Church falls between Man and God, Giotto's men enter directly into the sacred narrative as if it were their own life-story; the Godhead has descended into man and become his moral sense, no longer something to be adored in strict aloofness, but rather something immanent and active in the lives of men. There were two reasons for this new attitude. One of these was the example of St Francis, who had shown how the events of the life of Christ can be re-enacted here on earth; the other, the conditions of life in the Italian republics, which, with their struggles, their heroic deeds and their triumphs, encouraged men, greatly daring, to treat the divine mysteries as problems of morality.

Physical reality portrayed by means of plastic effects, and spiritual realities by illustration of the moral life—such are the two distinctive aspects of Giotto's style, and the base of his undying fame. But to achieve this reality, on the physical and spiritual planes, Giotto did not imitate nature, as all the later "realists" were to do. A man of the Middle Ages, he had all their fondness for the abstract line that, constricting bodies, endows them with a pent-up dynamism; for abstract form, which transmutes a mountain into a Rock of Ages; and for hierarchic proportion, which allots different sizes to figures according to the importance of the respective parts they play in the narrative. Thus the process of creation in Giotto's art was always from the abstract to the concrete. And, however visible the concrete element, it does not prevent our discerning in it the abstract values lying at its source. Those who study nature with an eye to idealizing it are incapable of that communion with the human soul which Giotto attains without the intermediacy of natural objects. All seems to come easily to him; all in his art is spontaneous, sincere, typical, essential. He goes straight to the soul, because he does not linger over the physical—and with such downrightness that in his work the soul seems indeed to constitute its whole reality. Thus in a flash of inspiration he conquered a new world, in which God and man were at one. But, as always happens in such cases, he lost something in so doing. Those fantastic, far-ranging flights of imagination we find in Cimabue had perforce to be restricted so as to enable the imagination to exercise itself within the limits set by man and to gain in depth what it lost in scope. Civilization was entering on the path its destiny assigned—of making man the master of this world below, by means of art to begin with, then by means of science.

Dante tells us it is well to forsake external beauty, so as to find another beauty that is all within, and in the light of these words we may compare Giotto with Duccio. To render his forms more spiritual, Giotto sacrificed the beauty to which Duccio was so faithful. The angel in the "Last Judgement" and the face of Christ confronting Caiphas have supreme moral, but not physical beauty. And it must be granted that an artist, who, with sympathy and love, explores the secret places of the soul, cannot— indeed, should not — linger on the beauty of the body. Nor did Giotto ornament his leading figures or assign decorative values to his groups; not arabesques, but the ideal structure of his compositions and figures was what interested him. Hence the unprecedented psychological complexity of his art; we cannot decide whether the angel has more strength than gentleness, Christ's face more nobility than humbleness. And whence comes the beauty of that angel of the "Judgement," save from his anguish, his pity for the poor doomed sinners?

Joachim is dreaming as he sleeps—lost in his dream, and it is on this the rhythms of the masses converge. Never does Giotto seek to delineate the moment when action is actually taking place; on the contrary, he concentrates on attitudes in which movement is implicit and potential, and it is these that give his works their pent-up vital energy.

His plastic realization of figures and objects is characterized by clean-cut outlines bringing each element into prominence, and is carried on within them by chiaroscuro. But Giotto refrains from the illusion of relief or sculpture in the round; his images are detached, but they do not "stand out." If he thus avoids relief, it is because he does not wish to stress the concrete, but, rather, aims at preserving that abstract quality in his portrayals which is implicit in the structure of his composition.

When Giotto started work at Assisi, the church had already been built and partially decorated; thus he had to adjust himself to a pre-determined lay-out. Also, he was still young and had not yet fully mastered his style. Nevertheless there is already in this work that forcefulness which was peculiarly his: powerful volumes and characteristic gestures like that, for instance, of St Francis preaching to the birds.

But when he entered the Scrovegni Chapel at Padua, he found at his disposal a large bare hall, not in any way built up. Thus he was at liberty to organize the surfaces as he thought fit, from floor to ceiling. Beginning from a plinth of imitation marble (with the figures of the Vices and Virtues in simili-relief), painted pillars run up to the vault and demarcate the blue zones above, strewn with golden stars and medallions of sacred figures, while below, in a triple line of frescos, are sacred scenes, ranging from the life of the Virgin's parents to Pentecost and the Last Judgement.

Hitherto painting had had to make shift with pre-determined architectural settings. But in this Chapel painting came into its own, made its own architecture, and imposed its own structural values, thus declaring the painter's independence as regards the architect.

Duccio narrates, Giotto represents. And since he belongs to the Middle Ages, this representation takes the form of pictures each of the nature of a transcendent vision; thus in them movement is symbolized, action merely suggested. Yet, even so, such is the expressive intensity of Giotto's work that inevitably it is dramatic.

"Joachim and the Shepherds" is a masterpiece of plastic art; the very rocks seem impregnated with a strange vitality of their own. Yet, with all its obvious and direct appeal to our aesthetic sense, we cannot overlook the emotive intensity of the shepherds' wonder and Joachim's bewilderment and distress. Thus, too, in the "Kiss of Judas" and the scene of the Mother mourning over her dead Son we have very human dramas of incomparable poignancy. Here souls are laid bare and emotions rendered by lines which, while owing nothing to any experienced reality, express everything by their own inherent power. It is the architecture of these two works that imparts a curiously fantastic quality to the dramatic events they illustrate: the lances *and torches above the heads of the surging group, and, in the "Pietà", the lay-out of verticals and horizontals cleft by the sloping transverse line of the rock that takes its rise above the head of the dead Christ.*

After his work at Padua Giotto painted the Santa Croce Church at Florence. And once again his style renewed itself. We have only to compare the sorrowing monks beside St Francis' deathbed with the Marys weeping the death of Christ. Though at Santa Croce Giotto has lost much of his dramatic intensity, this is counterbalanced by a new spontaneous charm in the gestures, more effective foreshortenings, and a broadened outlook on human life.

"St Francis receiving the Stigmata" (at Santa Croce) is, even for Giotto, a masterpiece of quite outstanding excellence. If we compare it with "Joachim and the Shepherds" we find that at Padua the vital force is more concentrated, whereas at Florence Giotto has given his imagination freer play. Thus St Francis' gesture, like the shape of the rock, is not absolutely necessary but is there simply to gratify the painter's imagination—and here we have a type of beauty hitherto unknown to art.

Assisi, Padua, Florence; these names mark three stages of Giotto's creative activity, three different conceptions of art. At Assisi he was trying to break loose from the tradition of Cimabue and, in general, from that of Byzantium. At Padua he took over from Gothic culture whatever served his ends—the humanization of divine figures, the use of plastic form and bright colour in the portrayal of religious subjects—, and created a new kind of Gothic art, thus anticipating the culture Florence was soon to give the world. At Florence the wheel has come full circle; while handling forms with serene mastery, he does not disdain the promptings of his imagination.

XIVth-century Florentine writers tell us that the "School of Giotto" included a great number of artists, and we have many frescos and pictures whose style obviously derives from his. But the actual names of only three are known to us: Taddeo Gaddi, Bernardo Daddi and Maso. The last-named was a very fine artist; more fantastic and more enigmatic, he differs greatly from his master. Ghiberti tells us he "abridged" the art of painting. By this he means that Maso did not depict all the elements of a scene in their entirety, but, by the use of "gaps" left the observer's fancy free to create what was omitted. This art of implications was, in the XIVth century, something quite exceptional. His masterpiece is a fresco showing two of St Sylvester's miracles; it gives a view of ancient Rome in ruins which is strikingly modern in conception. And another picture (rightly, it seems) attributed to him, and endowed with a singular fantastic power, brings out the difference of temperament and aim between him and his master. We might say that Maso restored to the dusk of mystery that which Giotto had illuminated with the light of truth.

GIOTTO (1267-1337).   ST FRANCIS PREACHING TO THE BIRDS.   FRESCO, UPPER CHURCH OF S. FRANCESCO, ASSISI.

GIOTTO

As once to Virgil's, an aura as it were of magic clings to Giotto's name and personality, and many were the legends that grew up round him, the tales told of his amazing precocity and the spell cast on contemporaries by his art. Indeed all the writers of his time, famous poets and prosaic chroniclers alike, spoke of him in terms of almost extravagant enthusiasm, and from the XVth century onwards he was universally acclaimed as being the one man who, by the magical power of his genius, delivered painting from the darkness of the Middle Ages. To-day his works can be identified with certainty, and enough of them have withstood the ravages of time for us to form a good idea of his qualities as an artist. As for his life, the information at our disposal, though limited to bare facts, is enough to give a notion of its chief landmarks and to tell us something of the real man, as apart from the almost mythical figure of his " legend."

Giotto was born in 1267 at Colle Vespignano, near Florence. The story goes that, as a shepherd boy, he was fond of making sketches of the sheep he tended. One day Cimabue chanced to pass by when he was thus drawing on a stone slab and, wonderstruck by the beauty and lifelikeness of the boy's work, took him to Florence to study in his *bottega* as an apprentice. Unfortunately, charming as this story is, the only part of it we can wholly rely on is that which vouches for Giotto's peasant origin and his attachment to the soil. Writing of Giotto, Ruskin has much to say of the poetic beauty of the countryside near Florence, its marvellous serenity and the soft, warm light bathing the silence of its pasture-lands. Born of this soil, Giotto imparted to his art something of the stability and tranquil power of unspoilt nature.

There is still much uncertainty as to his activities during his youth ; all we know for certain is that his first commissions were for work at Assisi, Rimini and Padua.

In the course of the XIIIth century two churches, one above the other, were built over the tomb of St Francis at Assisi, his birthplace. The Lower Church is entirely in the Romanesque style, with low piers and criss-cross vaulting, and, as a result, very dimly lit ; the Upper Church is in the French Gothic style with slender ribs and pointed vaulting fully lit by spacious windows.

Both churches were adorned with frescos : by Cimabue, by the Sienese Pietro Lorenzetti and Simone Martini, by Giotto and by his pupils. It has been no easy matter deciding, on the strength of the existing records, which frescos exactly were done by Giotto, and there was once much controversy on this subject. However, to-day it is generally agreed that the paintings in the Upper Church illustrating the Saint's life are from his hand ; with the exception of the last four scenes in which we find a more emphatically decorative style and which are probably the work of pupils, not of the master himself. This view rests on statements made by Riccobaldo da Ferrara (writing around 1312), in turn confirmed by Ghiberti and Vasari.

Giotto divided his frescos into twenty-eight parts, each approximately three yards square. Beginning from the right of the nave, with the prelude to the sainthood of St Francis, the story is carried on along the full length of the wall and continued along the wall on the left. The scene of *St Francis preaching to the Birds* is immediately to the left of the entrance door facing the nave.

Noteworthy is the manner in which Giotto has infused new life into a theme so often treated by artists of the XIIIth century. By isolating the Saint from the other elements of the picture, Giotto has succeeded in bringing into visual prominence the spiritual force embodied in St Francis ; this was quite a new development, in fact Giotto was doing for painting what was done, for poetry, by Dante who had the same end in view. This scene is not a mere illustration of the *Fioretti* ; Giotto saw in the *povero* of Assisi an incarnation of his own ideal.

GIOTTO (1267-1337). SCROVEGNI DONATING THE CHAPEL. DETAIL FROM THE LAST JUDGEMENT. FRESCO, SCROVEGNI CHAPEL, PADUA.

The style of this fresco indicates the transitional stage between Romanesque and Gothic. In the handling of the colours, especially, we see the painter keeping to the Cimabue tradition ; all trace of which was to disappear in the Padua frescos. Based on a somewhat forced interpretation of a tercet by Dante, running as follows,

Credette Cimabue nella pittura   (Cimabue thought to hold the field
Tener lo campo, ed ora ha Giotto il grido   In painting, and now Giotto hath the cry,
Si che la fama di colui l'oscura   So that the fame of Cimabue is obscured.)

PURGATORIO, CANTO XI,

SCROVEGNI CHAPEL, PADUA.   INTERIOR.   SEEN FROM THE ENTRANCE.

54

SCROVEGNI CHAPEL, PADUA.   INTERIOR.   SEEN FROM THE CHOIR.

GIOTTO (1267-1337). ANGEL. DETAIL FROM THE LAST JUDGEMENT. FRESCO, SCROVEGNI CHAPEL, PADUA.

56

the view prevailed that the relationship between Cimabue and Giotto was that of master and pupil. But it is manifest that the two artists stood for different tendencies. Where Cimabue relied on the play of light and shade, Giotto uses chiaroscuro for the rendering of plastic values. Even in the Assisi frescos, which must be regarded as an early work, we find some trends emerging which are not only new but directly opposed to those of all Giotto's predecessors, and which are, indeed, a foretaste of the methods of approach which he was to develop to the full in later years. These stylistic elements, moreover, enable us to see the basic kinship between the Assisi frescos and those at Padua, and thus tend to confirm the attribution of the former to Giotto. Still it cannot be denied there has been much difference of opinion on this matter, and also that we have to make the big assumption that, during a period estimated at some ten years, a vast access of power came to the painter, all the more difficult to account for because we know nothing at all of his activities during this period. It is possible that some time in the early years of the XIVth century he went to Rome, where he might have met Dante, but on this point, too, there is no really conclusive evidence.

★

It is in the frescos of the Scrovegni (or " Arena ") Chapel at Padua that Giotto shows himself at his splendid best, and very fortunately this great work has reached us in a state of excellent preservation.

This Chapel, formerly included in the Scrovegni Palace, was built by Enrico Scrovegni to atone for the misdeeds of his father Reginaldo, who was so avaricious that Dante placed him in the seventh circle of hell, amongst the usurers.

In the year 1305, the Chapel was consecrated with due pomp and ceremony. Some maintain that Giotto had a hand in the structural design as well as in the decoration of the edifice. In any case the simplicity of the lay-out gave the painter a marvellous field of action. Lighted by windows let into the right-hand wall, the entire wall space could be painted by him as his fancy led him, the whole inner structure having obviously been planned with an eye to mural decoration.

The walls on both sides of the nave are covered with a series of 37 fresco " panels " arranged in lines. Each scene is separated from its neighbours by pilasters carried up into the vault. The monochrome plinth is adorned with figures imitating sculpture, of the Vices and Virtues. The blue vaulted ceiling is ornamented with golden stars and circular medallions *(tondi)*, and the uniform background of the frescos is of the same blue as the ceiling. The panels are arranged in three series of equal size, the topmost eleven scenes illustrating the story of Anna, Joachim and Mary. These are followed up in the triumphal arch facing the entrance, by two frescos, *The Eternal Father bidding Gabriel announce her Motherhood to Mary*, and below, *The Annunciation*.

The middle row contains scenes from the life of Christ, which likewise occupy eleven panels. The same arrangement holds for the lowest row, in which we see *The Passion and the Death of Christ*. Above the entrance is a big fresco of *The Last Judgement*; on the left we see Signor Enrico Scrovegni making the gift of the Chapel, which is being borne aloft to God by three allegorical female figures.

According to an old tradition, Dante was Giotto's guest at Padua while he was working on these frescos. Though unfortunately there is no historical foundation for this legend, it is significant, as throwing light on the vast prestige that this work has enjoyed from the earliest days. All the writers of the age, dumbfounded by this " miracle of art," concur in praising its entire fidelity to nature. And it is true that Giotto builds up a self-sufficient world, with its own laws and internal structure, all of whose elements are bound together and integrated by his deep religious feeling and inviolable faith. Moreover his amazing plastic sense endows not only the figures but every detail of the scene with that psychological, not merely visual, intensity of which he supremely has the secret. Thus in *Joachim with the*

GIOTTO (1267-1337).   ADORATION OF THE MAGI.   FRESCO, SCROVEGNI CHAPEL, PADUA.

Shepherds the emphasis given by the artist to the trees and rocks is not less than that given the figures, and this contributes to the emotional tension which Giotto aimed at imparting to the scene.   " It is a scene of sadness—simple, stern, austere, summed up in postures of rigidity ; all here is broken rhythms, as of sobs crushed down and passion without anger, and over all these broods a meditative calm, hushing the inner tragedy. "

This gift for tautening up forms and his assured mastery of his resources enabled Giotto to deepen the emotive significance of all he set his hand to—so much so that even in the but slightly ruffled cloak draping Joachim, who is asleep, his head resting on his knees, we seem to have intimations of the visions haunting his slumber.   Thus in that simple, massive form we perceive not merely the body of the father of the Virgin, but a figuration of his dream, the destiny awaiting him.   Elsewhere we find lighter tones, limpid and serene, as in the *Adoration of the Magi.*   The half-relief of the forms suggests a tendency towards idealization and the abstract, and the story is told in terms of movement, but a movement paradoxically made of halts and pauses. In a general way Giotto's characters live so intensely that their acts and gestures are arrested, as it were, in mid-course, so as to enable us to glimpse that vast inner world of feeling which gave rise to them. The Magdalen at Christ's feet throws her arms passionately forward, but it is, rather, the crouching, fallen body that proclaims her grief. In the *Kiss of Judas* the lines of the pointing lances and in the *Pietà* the slanting line of the mountain, carried down to the ground-level, localize the point of maximum emotion. This composition in depth owes nothing to perspective, but is, rather, organized by the diagonal. The bodies of the grief-stricken figures build up, with their masses, an almost horizontal line, which is emphasized by the vertical figures grouped at the sides, like the silent " chorus " in an ancient tragedy.

" Starting from abstract architectural exigencies, and progressing by way of compact realistic portrayals, unfaltering, well-defined acts of Will, the art of Giotto encompasses the whole universe and subjugates it to man, in so far as man is the consciousness of a God, ruler of Space and Time."

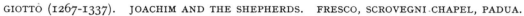

GIOTTO (1267-1337). JOACHIM AND THE SHEPHERDS. FRESCO, SCROVEGNI CHAPEL, PADUA.

GIOTTO (1267-1337). NOLI ME TANGERE (DETAIL). FRESCO, SCROVEGNI CHAPEL, PADUA.

Giotto was about forty when he finished painting the Scrovegni Chapel, and of all the works by him that have come down to us this is the best preserved as a whole; but there was no falling off in his activity after he left Padua. Some time before 1311 he was summoned to Rome by Cardinal Stefaneschi. The exact date of this visit and what work it involved are still moot questions. The documentary information regarding it is all of a trivial order; thus, in 1313 there is mention of his having trouble with his former landlady at Rome and trying to recover some bedding he had left with her.

An obituary notice, dated 1343, of Cardinal Stefaneschi tells of a " St Peter's Boat " in mosaic, and of a polyptych made by Giotto for the altar of this basilica in Rome. Unfortunately the mosaic was remade in the XVIIth century and its present condition leaves much to be desired. The polyptych, now in the Vatican Pinacoteca, is in a style somewhat different from that of his other work; probably Giotto supervised its making, but delegated the actual execution, for the most part, to apprentices of his *bottega*, as was a common practice in those days.

After his stay in Rome Giotto returned to Florence and set up house in the neighbourhood of S. Maria Novella, where he was working.

There must have been something uniquely stimulating in the intellectual and communal atmosphere of Florence, that city where, in a single generation, two such men as Dante and Giotto saw the light.

GIOTTO (1267-1337). JOACHIM'S DREAM (DETAIL). FRESCO, SCROVEGNI CHAPEL, PADUA.

GIOTTO (1267-1337). THE KISS OF JUDAS. FRESCO, SCROVEGNI CHAPEL, PADUA.

When, beginning in 1311, Giotto settled down to work there for several years and enrolled in the Guild of Physicians and Apothecaries (in which the painters were then included), Florence was already making good her dominance of Tuscany and asserting her independence as regards the King of Naples and the Emperor.

The government of the " Commune " or republic of Florence was based on the guilds of craftsmen, and fostered industrial and commercial ventures on the freest, most democratic lines that the conditions of the age permitted. But still more important is the fact that Florence was already beginning to sponsor a culture ever less cramped by the pedantry of the Universities, and favoured the stirring of new life manifest both in Dante's poems and in his friends' enthusiasm for the *dolce stil nuovo*.

While the power of Florence was at its height, over a number of years, the conflict between the old and the new ran its tumultuous course. The poets joined forces with the people and even took a hand in the government ; it was owing to this political activity that

Dante was banished, and remained in exile until his death, which took place at Ravenna in 1321. Giotto's activities at Florence were varied. He made a *Crucifix* for S. Maria Novella, a *Madonna Enthroned*, now at the Uffizi, for the Ognissanti Church, and a *Death of Mary*, now at Berlin.

He also did a great deal of work for the S. Croce Church, and four of its chapels were decorated by him. Two only of these fresco sequences have survived : that in the Peruzzi Chapel narrating the life of St John the Baptist and St John the Evangelist, and that in the Bardi Chapel, reverting to the theme of the Life of St Francis. Unhappily these frescos are in a deplorable condition ; overlaid with plaster for a long period, they were brought to light only in the XIXth century.

This may be regarded as the third great cycle of Giotto's frescos. Assisi showed us the personality of the artist as a quite young man ; at Padua we see him in full possession of his powers ; at Florence we have the style of his maturity, in which his youthful manner is visible, but recast in terms of a new ideal gradually built up during many creative years. The proportions show new tendencies towards elongation, figures and objects portrayed are set out in different planes ; thus they give a sense of mass existing in space and, if thereby

GIOTTO (1267-1337). PIETA. FRESCO, SCROVEGNI CHAPEL, PADUA.

GIOTTO (1267-1337). THE KISS OF JUDAS (DETAIL). FRESCO, SCROVEGNI CHAPEL, PADUA.

they lose in plastic power, they move more freely and fall into their respective places more harmoniously. The artist now seems less interested in literal portrayal. Whereas the protagonists of the Padua frescos lived dramatic lives, at Florence they seem more like dream figures ; here, too, the artist shows more concern for physical beauty than in his earlier work.

At Assisi Giotto's colour was still Byzantine ; at Padua, and still more so at Florence, it is Gothic—that is to say both lighter and more varied. And likewise the function of his colour has changed : at Padua it acts as a chiaroscuro, and contributes to accentuating plastic form. Thus, after reigning supreme for eight centuries, colour now yielded the palm to plastic form—a new development of far-reaching import, for not only did art thus proclaim its emancipation from Eastern influences, but now the way lay directly open to the art of modern times.

In January 1330 Giotto was at the Court of the King of Anjou at Naples. The King gave him the post of *Protomagister* (Master of Works) in respect of the decoration of the chapel in the Castel Nuovo (Royal Palace). This work, whose disappearance is a matter for keen regret to-day, was thought very highly of by the King who praised it in an Edict, and was also commended by Petrarch in his *Itinerarium Syriacum*.

Vasari has some anecdotes relating to Giotto's stay in Naples which illustrate the painter's keen and caustic humour ; the King, it seems, was greatly taken by his wit and the two men became good friends. In their romances, Boccaccio and, later, Franco Sacchetti often mention Giotto and describe him as a man with a taste for practical jokes and a gift for ready repartee. Still, what they show us of him is probably only one side of his character.

Giotto's stay at the Court of Naples lasted only a few years ; we learn that on April 12, 1334, he was back in Florence and appointed Master of the Works of the Cathedral *(Opera di Santa Riparata)*.   On July 18 of that year he started work on the foundations of the Campanile.

In this famous bell-tower and its lavish decorations, we see Gothic grace at its most exquisite.   It seems certain that Giotto supplied designs for some of its bas-reliefs, though actually these were carried out by Andrea Pisano.

Giotto did not live to see the completion of this edifice, whose proportions were criticized by the Florentines even in his lifetime.   He died at Florence on January 8, 1337, and was interred with pomp and circumstance in the Cathedral.

The following epitaph, inscribed under an effigy of Giotto, was composed by a humanist writer, Poliziano : " I am he by whose emprise the dead art of painting was restored to life ; whose hand was as faultless as it was compliant.   Nature herself lacked what was lacking in my art ; to none other was it given to paint more or better.   Dost thou admire that tower whence echoes the holy bronze ?   I designed it and 'tis following my design that thus it rises to the stars.   But what need for words ?   I am Giotto, and my name alone tells more than a long poem. "

It is impossible to overestimate Giotto's influence on art, and contemporary records

THE VARIATIONS OF INTENSITY IN THE BLUE BACKGROUNDS OF THE FRESCOS ARE DUE TO THE FACT THAT THOSE FACING THE WINDOWS HAVE SLIGHTLY FADED WHEREAS THOSE IN SHADOW HAVE KEPT THEIR ORIGINAL COLOUR.

GIOTTO (1267-1337).   PIETA (DETAIL).   FRESCO, SCROVEGNI CHAPEL, PADUA.

GIOTTO (1267-1337). ST FRANCIS RECEIVING THE STIGMATA. FRESCO, CHURCH OF S. CROCE, FLORENCE.

tell of many artists who were his disciples, though in some cases only their names are known to us.   Amongst those whose paintings have come down to us, are Taddeo Gaddi and Bernardo Daddi, both masters of the first rank ; and many of their paintings are extant. But as regards the greatest of them, Maso di Banco, we have to rely largely on the admiration of his contemporaries, for very few works by him have survived.

MASO From the year 1343 onwards there figures in the list of members of the Guild of Physicians and Apothecaries at Florence the name of Maso di Banco. "He was the most refined of all Giotto's pupils and his sense of beauty was truly prodigious." Thus wrote Filippo Villani in the XIVth century, and in the following century Ghiberti, too, has something to say of this painter, and tells us the St Sylvester frescos were his work.

But our information regarding this artist is lamentably meagre and, as if to make confusion worse confounded, Vasari attributes Maso's works to one "Tomaso di Stefano di Giottino"—an amalgam of two painters' names and that of a sculptor of a later date!

Still, much as we may regret that so little is known about the life of this distinguished artist, as compensation we have a few large-scale works, giving an excellent idea of his approach to art and his achievement. These are his frescos illustrating the life of St Sylvester, in the last chapel on the left of the altar of the S. Croce Church at Florence. In one of these we see Rodolfo dei Bardi, who commissioned these decorations, appearing at the Last Judgement. Evidently some dispute arose between the painter and the donor, for in 1341 Maso's property was sequestered at the behest of Signor Bardi. The most elaborate composition in the group is that which depicts the saint closing the dragon's jaws and recalling the dead to life ; and two scenes are included in the same panel, following a practice current in the Middle Ages, of illustrating more than one incident in a single composition. While the setting of both incidents is real enough—the Roman Forum—what strikes us in this picture is the way in which the artist has turned his back on any logical arrangement. Indeed a peculiar distribution of his figures and his technique of skilfully placed " accents " create an atmosphere at once highly original and fantastic. Evidently Ghiberti had this in mind when he remarked that Maso " greatly abridged " the art of painting. His abbreviations are not those impressions dear to our XIXth-century painters ; rather they tend to create an " unreal " space around the figures. Notable, too, is the way Maso accentuates a certain refinement in the faces—a procedure which might suggest affinities with Sienese art, especially with that of Ambrogio Lorenzetti. Nevertheless the sense of austere dignity we feel in his figures assimilates him rather to Giotto. While the dramatic element is not pitched in the same key, the imaginative freedom shown in handling it is more pronounced. We find the same characteristics in an *Entombment* now in the Uffizi, and marked " Giottino. " Though it would be rash to make any positive ascription, we certainly find in this work the same effect of mystery. The normal lay-out of the historical incident is here abolished, the donors mingle freely in the dramatic action on the religious plane, a thorough-going decentralization of the figures stresses the poetic intensity of the *ensemble,* and vivid colours on an abstract gold background contribute to the dream-like quality of the whole. Unfortunately even Ghiberti knew of very few works by this artist, and we, too, must remain content with this mere pittance of his output.

MASO (FIRST HALF OF XIVth CENT.). MIRACLES OF ST SYLVESTER. FRESCO, CHURCH OF S. CROCE, FLORENCE.

MASO (FIRST HALF OF XIVth CENT.).   PIETA   (77 × 53″)
UFFIZI, FLORENCE.

THE SIENESE

Though his masterpiece, the "Maestà" of Siena Cathedral, was painted some years later than Giotto's (in the Scrovegni Chapel), Duccio was the elder of the two artists. The generation following his at Siena produced three fine painters: Simone Martini, Pietro and Ambrogio Lorenzetti. And the "climate" these three men created for Siena was superior to that which Florence owed to the generation following Giotto. Then, beginning with the middle period of the XIVth century, the standard of the works of art produced in both cities, Florence and Siena, declined simultaneously. So much so that, towards the close of the century, we have to look to Padua, and Altichiero's art, to find work of outstanding value. It was not until the beginning of the XVth century that the great revival of Florentine art began.

It may be that all three Sienese masters of the first half of the XIVth century owed much to Duccio, and that the two Lorenzettis were also affected by the revolutionary changes introduced by Giotto. Nevertheless so personal were their styles that it would be rash definitely to speak of "influences."

We have already pointed out that while Duccio's approach to the Divine involved the mediation of the Church, Giotto established a direct, unmediated relationship between God and Man—not, indeed, man the individual, but mankind. The three Sienese artists likewise established contact between God and man, but "man" for them was the living individual, conditioned by his temporal environment. Thus for Simone Martini he was the aristocrat, member of an élite, the "perfect courtier" of the Middle Ages. For the Lorenzetti brothers he was the burgher who now held the reins of power at Siena, and, while eager to extend his wealth and prestige on the worldly plane, desired also to enlarge his mystical experience on the transcendental.

Both Simone Martini and Ambrogio Lorenzetti are worshippers of beauty, which they regard as the supreme refinement of mind and soul, partaking both in the religious sentiment of the Middle Ages and in the Neo-Platonism of the Renaissance. In this respect they differ obviously, and vastly, from Giotto.

All three artists have a great liking for the decorative, for ornamentation and the arabesque, which Giotto, ever in quest of that secret and supernal beauty whose source is holiness, banned from his art. Simone Martini and Pietro Lorenzetti had none of his reticence and "let themselves go" in a manner often verging on the "outré." Thus their style is uneven, over-wrought; yet, on occasion, it attains transcendence. Like Giotto all three started off from the abstract and often they did not get beyond it (this is especially true of Simone); but they never effected that harmonious and total synthesis of reality which we find in the masterpieces of the Florentine. Nevertheless they succeeded, often better than he, in coming close to certain aspects of reality. Indeed it is they (Simone Martini in particular) who inaugurated that realistic treatment of details which is so characteristic of the international style of the beginning of the XVth century and the Northern Renaissance.

We may add that the brothers Lorenzetti had a grasp of linear perspective much superior to Giotto's, and that they render landscape in a manner both more objective and more elegant than his. In this field, indeed, they show leanings towards a virtuosity which, while attractive, is far indeed from Giotto's austere self-restraint.

It was in their colour that the Sienese unequivocally excelled. Already Duccio had created a chromatic style that could hold its own beside the Byzantine mosaics and Gothic stained glass; Simone and the Lorenzetti brothers developed this style to a point that has never been surpassed. At once complex and refined, it is infused with an amazing sensibility, and Giotto's colouristic methods, perfect in their own way as they are, seem rudimentary compared with theirs.

Simone belongs to the Gothic decorative tradition which found supreme expression chiefly in the work of the illuminators, whereas the Lorenzettis may be ascribed to the Gothic expressionist tradition, which had already produced some masterpieces in sculpture (for example that of Giovanni Pisano). Giotto likewise belonged to Gothic culture, but he created his own type of Gothic, outside any tradition.

Thus the achievement of Siena during the first half of the XIVth century ranks very high in the history of art; it teems with surprising discoveries and displays an almost limitless imaginative freedom. Yet somehow the more we admire it, the more we feel Giotto's unique eminence.

Simone Martini was a friend of Petrarch, illustrated his "Virgil," and painted his Laura's portrait. He was also persona grata at the Court of Anjou at Naples and at that of the Popes at Avignon. The elegance, refinement and (not to mince words) snobbery of the Sienese aristocracy found in him an ideal interpreter. In his imagination he assimilated the Courts of Love and the Court of Heaven, the result being that his mysticism has a slightly mundane tinge. One can hardly conceive of a more refined figure than that of his Gabriel in the Uffizi "Annunciation"; so handsome, so obviously well-bred is he. No painted form perhaps has ever had so much of the "jewel" about it as this; though, needless to say, we may question if the highest aim of painting is to turn out jewellery.

The decorative value of the "Annunciation" lies in its adaptation of the thematic material to the Gothic arches marking the divisions of the surface. That there may be constructive values never crossed Simone's mind. The quality of his art consists in his undulating line set off by surfaces of richly glowing colour, brilliant as enamel-work. His love of jewel-like effects, his facile self-surrender to the rhythms of his flowing lines evidence his sensuality, which, nevertheless, he refines and sublimates on to a spiritual plane in a manner which compels our admiration.

Guidoriccio da Fogliano was a condottiere in the service of Siena; we are shown him visiting on horseback his castles, his entrenchments and his troops. So much for the historical data. What more have we here? The poetry of the rippling line which unites in the same rhythm rider, horse and landscape. This is a fairy-tale, unconcerned with the realities of war, and fancy-free as a minstrel's song.

Towards the end of his career Simone felt a need to renew himself, to forge for himself a new reality, and the Stefaneschi polyptych, painted at Avignon, testifies to this endeavour. He has at his command the subtlest procedures, the technique of the most delicate rendering of figures, and now he wishes to use this hoarded knowledge for the expression of intense sorrow, rugged force, even violence. Perhaps the contrast between his resources and his new ideal makes itself felt here and there; yet this injection of energy and vital force proved beneficial. We have already mentioned Duccio's incapacity for rendering a dramatic scene; the same is true of Simone Martini. Yet we feel in his art that he has tendencies to the dramatic and takes them seriously. This it is that gives their moral content to his dainty colour-effects and courtly graces, and brings a vivifying breath of reality into the closed world of the aristocracy. Though a realism of detail only, it is very much alive; it both infused new life into Gothic in its decline and prepared the way for the Northern Renaissance.

It is not known which of the Lorenzetti brothers was the elder; however, the obvious affinities between Pietro, in his early works, and Duccio suggest that it was he. Also we find in his art an austerity both of form and spirit which is absent in his brother Ambrogio's work, as in that of Simone.

The most striking characteristic of Pietro is his dramatic power; thus we may regard him as unique amongst the Sienese and liken him to Giotto. It is neither grace nor refinement that predominates in his art; he is highly strung, fantastical, and indulges in extravagances of expression, which, however, he transmutes into absolute values. Thus, in his "Virgin and Child," he does not aim at charm, nor at expressing the love of mother and child, or the divine nature of the figures. He reads into their attitude towards each other a precognition of their tragic destinies; in the Son's eyes the Madonna sees the cross and death, and the Son is casting a questioning gaze at his Mother, as if seeking to learn from her what the future holds in store. All this is expressed by an undulating line, but how far removed from the dreamy, smoothly flowing modulations of Simone Martini! Here the line is thronged with the accents of tragedy, vibrant with anguished apprehension.

His masterpiece, which is also the most poignantly tragic work of the whole century, is his "Descent from the Cross." In this fresco the painter has taken yet a bolder forward step. Carried away by his emotion, he has distorted the body of Christ; so that it may cover the space needed to give its utmost expression to the anguish of the suffering Redeemer, he lends the body a stature justified only by the exigencies of its spiritual import, the length of the figure enabling its contortions to make their full effect.   And in this supreme spasm of physical pain the body of Christ assumes the form of a bent bow which, by a prodigy of art, unifies the whole composition.

Giotto had achieved equilibrium in the "Pietà" by the interplay of verticals and horizontals.   Pietro Lorenzetti casts all his figures into the crucible of his emotion and his structural form derives from the emotive unity of all the elements.

The monumental quality of his art and the grandeur of his conceptions are strikingly illustrated by a detail which might well have been a mere "genre" piece— the two serving-women bringing the water and linen for the birth of Mary; Pietro Lorenzetti makes the two servants two monuments to human dignity.

The Lorenzetti brothers painted some superb landscapes.   We see one of these, by Pietro, in a predella, representing the Fountain of Elias whence the Carmelites are drawing water.   It is a scene of everyday life in a rocky country.   The treatment of the rocks is very near Giotto's; yet they are less detached, and merge more fully into the composition as a whole because the zones of light and shade are indicated by colour rather than by chiaroscuro.

In another landscape, this time on the seashore (ascribed, rightly in my opinion, to Ambrogio Lorenzetti), we may note that not only are the colour contrasts less pronounced but the contour of the hill has no longer the starkness of drawing pure and simple; it arises from the colour itself.   Here we have a masterpiece that, outstripping the taste of its century, foreshadows Piero della Francesca.

But it is in Ambrogio Lorenzetti's religious works that his true greatness lies. His far-ranging imagination seems to move from contemplation of the landscape to that of the divine with equal ease, and with the same purity of heart.   His "Madonna Enthroned," if but a small picture, is a great one in achievement.   So as to enhance the splendour of the Madonna he does not hesitate to tamper with the true perspective line and to elevate, irrationally, the throne.   Here humility and grace find their supreme expression, and we have mysticism at its purest.   And how different a mysticism from that of Berlinghieri!   There is in Ambrogio Lorenzetti a profoundly human instinct forbidding him to see the divine otherwise than under aspects of grace and beauty—divinity at its loveliest.

Let us turn to "St Dorothy."   Amongst the many beautiful forms Ambrogio created, none other breathes a mystical exaltation so intense, or burns with a glow of faith so fervent.   The flowers, the shapely hands, the volumes of a perfectly formed body, the face at once gentle and severe—all these minor beauties are quenched in that gaze which is the very synthesis of beauty and of faith.

We know little of Ambrogio's life; it is said that he was a "philosopher" (that is to say, a cultured man), who took part in the literary, social and political activities of his country.   Indeed we seem to see intimations in his work of something more than the personality of an artist, even a very great one; something that, ranging beyond his painting, hints at hopes or aspirations—that came to nothing.   For the plague epidemic of 1348 which, it seems, carried off the Lorenzetti brothers—and from which dates the decadence of Siena—prevented Ambrogio from realizing that secret dream whose presence we feel disseminated through his works.

SIMONE MARTINI (CA. 1284-1344). ANNUNCIATION (DETAIL). 1333. UFFIZI, FLORENCE.

SIMONE MARTINI

Simone Martini belongs to the second generation of Sienese painters. The end of Duccio's life synchronizes, within a year or so, with the date ascribed to the first work by Simone Martini that has come down to us. Four years after Martini's death came the Great Plague, amongst whose victims were the brothers Pietro and Ambrogio Lorenzetti. And with that year began a decline in the quality of Sienese creative art.

Born at Siena, probably in 1283 or 1284, Simone Martini lived to enjoy and to admire that swelling tide of cultural achievement and material prosperity which in the first half of the fourteenth century made the name of Siena famous as the home of a civilization such as the world had rarely seen. The aristocracy had yielded the reins of power to a rich middle class composed of merchants and bankers, as was also the case at Florence. But though these towns were not far distant from each other, their cultures evolved on very different lines. Thus at Siena the aristocratic ideal lingered on over a long period, and the strain of poetic fancy which we find in Sienese art has qualities all its own. Nothing, indeed, could have been further from the rationalist, critical and " ethical " attitude to life of the Florentines. Indeed as early as the XVth century the philosophic trend of Florentine art, as against the poetic and literary qualities of the Sienese, was commented on.

We know nothing of the activities of Simone Martini before the year 1315, when the city of Siena commissioned him to paint a large *Maestà* for the Sala del Mappamondo at the Palazzo Pubblico. Remembering the enthusiasm with which four years previously the Sienese had acclaimed Duccio's *Maestà*, we may feel sure that when ordering a new work they engaged a painter in whose abilities they had the utmost confidence. This picture is now in a lamentable state; as a matter of fact we know that it deteriorated very rapidly, since on December 30, 1321, the Commune made a second payment to the artist, instructing him to revive its colours.

In 1317, two years after finishing the *Maestà*, Simone was invited to the Court of King Robert of Anjou, at Naples. For an emolument of 50 ounces of gold *per annum*, the king had him paint a picture commemorating his crowning by his brother, Louis, who had entered the Church.

About 1320 he was working for the towns of Pisa and Orvieto, each of which commissioned him to paint a polyptych (now to be seen in the collections of these towns).

1324 was an important year both as regards his career as an artist and for his private life. It was in this year that he married the daughter of the painter Memmo Memmi. Thus he became the brother-in-law of Lippo Memmi, with whom he often worked in collaboration. Another of the assistants in his *bottega* was his brother Donato.

Four years later Simone Martini was back in Siena, where he painted the equestrian portrait of Guidoriccio da Fogliano. This famous condottiere of the army of Siena had just brought off a brilliant victory over Castruccio Castracani, and such was the enthusiasm of the Sienese over this great feat of arms that they decided to have a picture commemorating it. Simone was asked to make it, and this fresco, which is dated, is still in the Palazzo Pubblico. This portrait has a dream-like, poetic quality, rare in works of this order. The picture shown us of the condottiere riding past, against a background of castles and entrenchments, as he inspects his defences on the eve of battle is less like the record of an historic scene than an episodic tale whose course we follow from right to left, as the action develops. The linear rhythm of the composition is twofold; while included in its own space bounded by flowing lines, the landscape is not included in the space in which the rider moves—he stands out, an isolated figure, against the background.

One of Simone's best known works is the *Annunciation* now at Florence, in the Uffizi. Dated 1333, this picture bears two signatures: of Simone Martini and Lippo Memmi. There has been much debate as to the share of each of the two artists in this work, but the general consensus of opinion to-day attributes the two saints at the sides to Lippo. Yet, whatever were their respective shares in it, there is no doubt that this picture not only displays all the characteristics of Simone's genius but that it ranks in itself as one of the peak-points of absolute art.

Here, the harmony between colour, line and psychological content is consummate. The gold background, which for the Middle Ages had a merely symbolical reference, here plays an active part in the colour-scheme. Indeed throughout the scene the colours have a marvellous translucence, the brilliance of illuminations in a Book of Hours, while the tremulously shrinking attitude of the Virgin, awestruck by the angel's message, is delightfully expressed in graceful undulations of the line. As in the Guidoriccio fresco, space is implicit in the movement of the action along the painted surface, but here figures and objects are segregated in the triple arches of the frame. The lay-out of the composition is prescribed by the architecture, irrelevant, in the last analysis, to the figure sequence. The amazing lavishness of decorative colour in the angel's garment and in the vase of gladioli, has made this fresco one of the most admired masterpieces of Italian art.

While at Siena Simone Martini was asked to undertake a mission to the Pope, and taking his wife and his brother Donato with him, he proceeded to Avignon (in 1339). He was destined never to return to his country. There are grounds for believing that he did much work, when attached to the papal court; but unhappily few of his mural paintings of this time have survived, and those that have are almost ruined. The chief event of his life during this period was his meeting with Petrarch, who was then living in retirement in the Vaucluse district, near Avignon.   His writings testify to his deep affection for the painter, and in some immortal lines he extols the portrait of Laura made by Simone Martini.   " Surely my friend Simone was once in Paradise, whence came this gentle lady ; then, having seen her there, he limned her face on paper to convince this world below of the beauty of her countenance. " This portrait is unfortunately lost to us.

Elsewhere Petrarch likens him to Zeus, Praxiteles and Pheidias.   And we can understand and, in some measure, share the poet's enthusiasm, when we look at Simone's pictures and mark how aptly grace of line and brilliancy of colour have been wedded by the artist's creative imagination.   It is not without good reason that they bring to our minds the curves of Gothic and a particular "climate" not uniquely Italian.   But the dazzling effects, the glorious colour and the extreme fondness Simone shows for gold, for gem-like lustre, for textures glittering with broken lights, seem almost to suggest influences hailing from the East, such as in fact are traceable in the work of other Sienese painters.

Of Simone's output during his Avignon period only two works (apart from the much damaged frescos in the Notre-Dame Church) remain : a *Holy Family* (at Liverpool) and the Stefaneschi polyptych, commissioned by the Cardinal of that name (who died in 1341) ; it was he who had asked Giotto to make for him the *St Peter's Boat* and the polyptych for St Peter's at Rome.   Simone's polyptych was divided into parts ; the *Annunciation, Crucifixion* and *Descent from the Cross* are in Antwerp, while the *Way to Golgotha* is in Paris, in the Louvre, and the *Pietà* in Berlin.   Likewise in the scenes of Christ's Passion we discern efforts towards a more dramatic form of expression, and the new feeling for reality and the power displayed in these works brilliantly supplement the decorative predispositions so apparent in Simone's style.

This, his " Avignon style, " bore fruit in the French illuminations of the last half of the XIVth century ; indeed its influence extended to the work of the Limbourg brothers, and thereby played no inconsiderable part in the Renaissance of the North.

SIMONE MARTINI (CA. 1284-1344). GUIDORICCIO DA FOGLIANO (DETAIL). FRESCO, PALAZZO PUBBLICO, FLORENCE.

SIMONE MARTINI (CA. 1284-1344). THE WAY TO GOLGOTHA. PART OF THE CARDINAL STEFANESCHI TRIPTYCH.
(10 × 4″) LOUVRE, PARIS.

SIMONE MARTINI (CA. 1284-1344).   DESCENT FROM THE CROSS.   PART OF THE CARDINAL STEFANESCHI TRIPTYCH.
(10″ × 4″)   ANTWERP.

PIETRO LORENZETTI

The ambition of the proud, high-spirited populace of Siena in the first half of the Trecento was to make their city supreme amongst all cities both in material wealth and in works of art. Thus, though their Cathedral had been satisfactorily completed at the close of the XIIIth century, they decided, jealous of the size of the Cathedral at near-by Orvieto, to enlarge it. (In 1357, however, owing to the stringency of the times, they had to call off work on it—which was perhaps as well, for the plans showed more enthusiasm than discretion.)

This, too, was the period when a second generation of painters was coming to the fore ; amongst them Simone Martini, whose Gothic delicacy was to revivify the fading elegance of an aristocratic world already on its decline, and the brothers Pietro and Ambrogio Lorenzetti whose temperaments were more in accord with the changing spirit of the time, and who set their course towards a new ideal.

It is recorded that these two painters were born at Siena, but we do not know which was the elder. In the records the first date referring to Ambrogio is 1319, and to Pietro,1320. (An entry for 1306 mentions a painter named " Petruccio di Lorenzo, " but not only is the name considerably different, but, were this really Pietro Lorenzetti, it would mean that he was many years older than Simone Martini—which is most unlikely.) Ghiberti says nothing of Pietro, though he has much to say of his brother, while Vasari, misreading a signature, mutilates even his name, and the biography he gives of Pietro in his *Lives* is vague and confused. Though trustworthy records are lacking, stylistic considerations point to Pietro's being the elder of the two : one of these being the fact that we clearly see the imprint of Duccio's style in Pietro's work, while there is no trace of it in Ambrogio's.

In 1320 Pietro painted a polyptych for the town of Arezzo, and there are records of a payment made him for paintings he did at this time for the Siena Cathedral. Nine years later he made a large *Madonna*, for the Carmine church at Siena, and on the predella are various scenes from the History of the Carmelites. One of these, *The Fountain of Elias*, is particularly interesting as we find in it a feature that Pietro was to develop in almost all his later work : emphasis given to the movement of figures in a landscape. When we remember Duccio's indifference in this respect, and Simone Martini's purely linear movement, it becomes evident that, in thus boldly rendering motion in space, Pietro took a great step forward.

Between 1333 and 1337 he was commissioned to paint a number of pictures, amongst them a fresco for Siena Hospital (in collaboration with his brother) ; but none of these has survived. At Florence there is a *Madonna Enthroned* by him, but its date is uncertain.

It is regrettable that so little information about this painter's life is forthcoming ; that the few mentions of him in chronicles of the periods are so scrappy and of such slight interest. Even the date of his death, rumoured to have taken place during the 1348 plague epidemic, cannot be verified.

Pietro did fresco decorations in the left transept of the Lower Church of S. Francesco at Assisi. Not all the paintings, which cover the walls up to the vaulting, can safely be attributed to him and even now there is no general consensus of opinion on the matter. But there is no question of the great interest of this work for lovers of art, nor can we fail to be struck by its strong emotive quality—especially in the *Madonna with two Saints* and the *Descent from the Cross*. Though Lorenzetti, too, owes much to Gothic art, the stylistic elements he takes from it are quite other than those we find in the work of Simone. It is not the decorative and linear aspects of the visible world that interest him, but the inner life of the heart. In his *Madonna and Child*, so poignant is the feeling of intimate affection and understanding between the two personages that this may be regarded as the first of those " Holy Families " which are named in Italian " sacred colloquies " because all the personages seem to be " conversing " with the Virgin and the Child.

(91 ½ × 129″)   FRESCO, LOWER CHURCH OF S. FRANCESCO, ASSISI.

PIETRO LORENZETTI (?-1348). MADONNA AND CHILD (DETAIL). FRESCO, LOWER CHURCH
OF S. FRANCESCO, ASSISI.

When we study his work as an *ensemble*, we perceive that in his desire to realize
intensity of expression he does not shrink from distorting linear patterns to that end, and
also that he gives an individual value to each element of the scene.

PIETRO LORENZETTI (?-1348). FOUNTAIN OF ELIAS. PART OF THE PREDELLA OF THE CHURCH OF
THE CARMINE, PISA. (35 ½ × 14 ½") PINACOTECA, SIENA.

In the fresco of the *Descent from the Cross*, effect is given both tendencies. The whole scene is built up in terms of the curve described by Christ's body, in whose arched line is concentrated the anguish of those surrounding Him. Contrasting with this curve, the straight line of the cross binds down the architecture of the scene, which as a whole gives the impression of an epitome of tragedy whence all that is not grief has been refined out of existence.

It is impossible to say if he was directly influenced by the work of Giotto ; what is certain is that the emphasis he gives to the " action " of the scene portrayed brings him nearer the work of the sculptor Giovanni Pisano. Indeed no other fresco displays quite the impassioned, dramatic intensity so evident in this *Descent from the Cross*, though in other works by this painter we observe similar linear movements and the same determination of the lay-out by the psychological situation.

The last painting ascribed with certainty to Pietro is a panel dated 1342 showing the *Nativity of the Virgin*, now in the Opera del Duomo at Siena. This work is in three parts, but the painter has not kept to the division imposed by the structure of the triptych ; the scene between the second and third compartments is consecutive, we feel it continuing beyond the arches intersecting it. There is both grace and strength in the figures of the two servants on the right; though forming part of the *ensemble*, they tell out like independent portraits. The direct emotional appeal of Piero's art is unmistakable and many XIVth-century painters, even outside Siena, were strongly influenced by it.

PIETRO LORENZETTI (?-1348). DESCENT FROM THE CROSS.

PIETRO LORENZETTI (?-1348). BIRTH OF THE VIRGIN (DETAIL).
OPERA DEL DUOMO, SIENA.

AMBROGIO LORENZETTI (?-1348).   MADONNA ENTHRONED.   (19 × 12 ½″)
PINACOTECA, SIENA.

AMBROGIO LORENZETTI

We know that Ambrogio, Pietro's brother, was born at Siena, but there is no record of the date of his birth. The first indication of his activities is a picture dated 1319 ; two years later he enrolled in the Painters' Guild at Florence. Between 1319 and 1332 he divided his time between Florence and Siena ; he is known to have been at the latter town in 1331, painting frescos in the Church of S. Francesco.

Though records of the time and the material collated by Vasari fail to give us any clear idea of the personality of Pietro Lorenzetti, we have somewhat better information regarding his brother Ambrogio.

Ghiberti, while omitting all mention of Pietro, speaks of Ambrogio as the painter nearest to his heart, and Vasari remarks that in his work he produces rather the impression of a man of good breeding and high culture than that of an artist. Here Vasari is echoing the tradition according to which Ambrogio was a man of letters as well as a painter, frequented the society of poets and also took a hand in politics. The only fact we know, in this connexion, is that towards the close of his life he delivered a public lecture ; but it is not stated whether its theme was art or politics. Though we must go warily in accepting all that Vasari tells us, we certainly feel the presence of a refinement, new to the age, in this painter's art, and likewise a tendency towards expression of a more abstract order than that in his brother Pietro's work. There are obvious affinities of style between the two brothers, yet the personality behind Ambrogio's work is quite distinctive ; it may be regarded as a brilliant synthesis of tendencies prevailing in the world of art over more than half a century.

That emotional vehemence which characterized his brother had no place in Ambrogio's responses to the visible world ; he transformed the passionate, dramatic presentation of the subject which came so naturally to Pietro, into a non-dramatic poetry, whose nobility and very real sense of grandeur transcend the human element. As regards style, Ambrogio, like his brother, achieved an exceptional vividness of expression by aiming not only at using space as a setting for figures and objects, but also at using these figures and objects to emphasize the effect of spatial recession.

The outstanding quality of Ambrogio's art is, doubtless, its mysticism, a mysticism of rare intensity, which he expresses with serene conviction, an unfailing sense of the sublime.

It would be pleasant could we see, as Ghiberti saw them, those frescos in the Church of S. Francesco at Siena, which are amongst Ambrogio's earliest works. Unhappily they have come down to us in very bad condition. Nevertheless the scenes that have survived are of the utmost interest, particularly for the light they throw on the painter's new conception and handling of space.

During his stay in Florence Ambrogio painted frescos and an altarpiece for St Nicolas' Chapel in the Church of S. Procolo. The former no longer exist but there are in the Uffizi some panels, narrating the Legend of St Nicolas, which probably formed part of the altarpiece. What strikes us in these scenes is the freedom of the representation. Thus the scene here reproduced, of the *Miracle of the Corn*, has a delightful vivacity and unconstraint. And the *Madonna, Saints, and Angels* brings out still more clearly the wealth of colour, so typically Sienese, in Ambrogio's art. For all its small dimensions, this picture is undoubtedly one of the loftiest visions of divinity that has ever been vouchsafed an artist. Its construction in depth has won universal admiration. The place assigned each figure has been carefully thought out with a view to giving the composition a sequence of planes receding into the gold of the sky. The saints kneeling at the foot of the throne, acting as " supporters " of the central scene, and the angels receding horizonwards and merging into the golden distance, as they escort the Madonna and Child in their ascent—all these figures play their part in the construction of the whole ; while the colours—a counterpoint of gleams of gold and luminous, variegated hues—seem joining in a hymn of praise to the enthroned Madonna. Few painters have rendered so superbly this atmosphere of high festival on the celestial plane. This work

AMBROGIO LORENZETTI (?-1348). A CASTLE BY THE SEA. (8¾ × 12 ½")
PINACOTECA, SIENA.

is generally attributed to the painter's last phase, but no precise date can be assigned. The same is true of the St Dorothy triptych at the Siena Museum. Here, too, the serene, mystical rapture illuminating the saint's face is such as could be imparted only by an artist at once profoundly human and ever seeking to draw nearer that Absolute which transcends the human.

Despite his mysticism and devotion to religious subjects, a major work by Ambrogio Lorenzetti deals with a social theme. This is the sequence of frescos in the Sala della Pace at Siena (painted some time between 1337 and 1339). The contemporary renown of the artist and of Sienese painting in general is often attributed to these frescos. It may be that the subject had much to do with their popularity, but there is no question of their value as works of art on every count. Their theme is *Good and Bad Government* and *The Effects of Good Government*. These frescos, which form a sequence covering three walls, give a series of realistic glimpses of everyday life, and some symbolical scenes, not without a propagandist bias. Similar subjects were often treated in the XIVth century in Italy, and Giotto is known to have painted something on these lines for the Mayoral Palace at Florence, but no trace of it remains.

These frescos are much the worse for the lapse of time. But though we get only a poor idea of the original colours, enough remains to illustrate the idealism, at once poetic and political, which tradition has ascribed to the painter.

We find again this intricate rendering of planes, so characteristic of Ambrogio, in a fragment *Castle by the Sea*, which probably formed part of a panel now lost. In a good state of preservation, it gives an excellent idea not only of the richness of this great artist's colour but also of his conception of space and of his intimate feeling for nature.

After this work on a sociological theme, for which he was handsomely remunerated, Ambrogio Lorenzetti made the statue of an angel and a chandelier for the Madonna of the Siena Cathedral and in 1340 he was paid the considerable sum of 135 gold florins for an altarpiece, also commissioned by the Cathedral. Two later pictures by him are extant: the *Presentation in the Temple* (1342), now at the Uffizi, and an *Annunciation* (1344) at Siena. It is believed that Ambrogio, and his brother Pietro, died in the plague epidemic of 1348.

After the death of this great artist the creative genius of the Sienese seems to have fallen on a decline. The plague epidemic had a disastrous effect, carrying off as it did many of Siena's most promising talents. But before the close of the XIVth century one painter with an outstanding personality emerged—we have Barna in mind—as well as several minor but attractive artists. None the less the prestige of this Italian city which gave so many art treasures to the world was, to all intents and purposes, at an end.

AMBROGIO LORENZETTI (?-1348). THE MIRACLE OF THE CORN. FROM THE LEGEND OF ST NICHOLAS. (18 ½ × 20″) UFFIZI, FLORENCE.

AMBROGIO LORENZETTI (?-1348).   ST DOROTHY : DETAIL FROM THE ST DOROTHY TRIPTYCH.
PINACOTECA, SIENA.

THE CLOSE
OF THE MIDDLE AGES

There are three different ways of escape, as the famous Dutch historian Huizinga has observed, from our afflictions here below: one is to believe in a better world beyond the grave, the second to take active steps to better the world we live in, the third to dream oneself into a world of fairy-tale. The men of the late Middle Ages chose the third way out, and this choice by its very nature favoured the development of the plastic arts.

Also to be noted is the fact that the independent "Communes" had had their day, and everywhere the power had passed into the hands of the noble families. At all these Courts (most brilliant of which was that of Burgundy) there was a great demand for painters capable of providing that thrill of pleasure which comes from the spectacle of imagined beauty. And the painters, generously treated by their noble patrons, gladly applied themselves to implementing the ideal of elegance and dignity, touched with "bizarrerie," that these patrons called for.

Thus the social and political conditions of the time did much to promote the rise of that flamboyant Gothic style which, spreading over Europe, became known as the international style. That Italy took so active a part in this art movement was due largely to Simone Martini. Representing as he did the fine flower of aristocratic taste, he influenced not only Italian artists but also those practising at the courts of Burgundy and Le Berry. Nevertheless this international tendency met with opposition at Florence, where a venture very different and on every count far more important was under way.

Moreover it was in the north of Italy that Italian art approximated most closely to that of Burgundy; thus it is not surprising that the two early XVth-century painters in whose art the refinement, lavish adornment and imaginative beauty characteristic of the "international style" are most apparent, did not hail from Florence. Gentile da Fabriano came from the region of Italy where Raphael was later to be born, and Pisanello (though Pisa was his birthplace) looked for his inspiration to the North. Both had highly successful careers, with the Pope, Venice and the greatest princes vying for their services.

*In " The Adoration of the Magi," his masterpiece, Gentile da Fabriano com-
bines the oriental lavishness of his visual imagination with an innate Italian grace;
we find the former in the garments of the Magi, the latter in the faces of the youths
and women.   Even the old men have something of the softly moulded forms and
bloom of youth.   His ideal is the Prince Charming, and, despite his realism, his
world is the world of fairy-tale.   The truth is that realism and mediaeval art went
quite well together.   And, like that of Jan van Eyck, Gentile's art, at once skilful
and meticulous, transports us into a realm of exotic dreams.*

*Pisanello, who is believed to have been one of Gentile's pupils, outdid his master
not in the representation of grace and beauty, but in imaginative scope; as we see
in his " St George" and " St Eustachius."   Moreover he gave his propensity for
realism yet freer play in certain portraits and in his medals, which are amongst the
finest the world has seen.*

*It is with his line that he brings out character in the portrait of " Lionello
d'Este"; indeed the graphism is the making of this portrait, and its predominance here
reminds us of Gothic art.   But, with Pisanello, it has such dynamism, such compactness, and brings out plastic form so powerfully that we feel tradition counts for nothing;
here the artist's native genius is all.   This portrait suggests the path by which, had
it not been for Florence, the Italians would have gradually advanced towards the
Renaissance.   Paradoxical as this may seem, the more this artist concentrates on
objectivity in his representation, the more it takes on that dream-like quality to which
his art owes its singular enchantment.*

*There are two links between him and the Middle Ages; starting from an abstract
lineal pattern, he enriches it with colours and nuances until it gives an illusion of the
real, and at the same time he never loses sight of the ideals of chivalry and exquisite
manners of an aristocratic world which would soon have either to transform itself or
pass away.   Nevertheless there is also a link, if an indirect one, between him and the
Renaissance: the vital energy, the creative vigour he puts into his plastic images.
Indeed this opened the way to developments of the most varied kinds—with the one
exception of that drastic revolutionary swerve which led to the Renaissance.*

*Even at Florence the revolutionary spirit was exceptional.   Lorenzo Monaco,
for instance, was a great artist, and recognized as such by his contemporaries; nevertheless he never consciously thought of altering the Gothic tradition.   In practice,
though abiding by it, he did modify it—by exaggerating the undulations of his line and
imparting to them nuances so delicate that light seems streaming out of them.   His
conception of the divine suggests a retrogression, to as far back as Duccio; between
God and his imagination always the Church intervenes.   In his great altarpieces the
formal portrayal and the very perfection of the craftsmanship suppress almost entirely
the artist's personality.   Indeed he would seem to be more an illuminator than a painter; and one of the characteristics of illumination is the high place given to technical
perfection.*

Yet we glimpse behind this monastic reticence and painstaking craftsmanship a very great sensibility, which, despite their formalism, shines through in the predellas and the small pictures. Thus we realize the tender emotion aroused in him by the Virgin adoring the Child, the mystical despair into which the thought of Calvary has plunged him, the element of the miraculous that he perceives in the daily life of the monks, and the craving he feels to bathe all things in the light of the divine.

Tradition may act as a brake—yet how much Lorenzo Monaco owed to it, and not least a formal self-restraint calling for spirituality of a high order!

While Pisanello bodies forth an aristocratic ideal, that of the most refined Court in Italy, Lorenzo Monaco, on the other hand, stands for the religious spirit of the convents, interpreted on its highest level and with complete sincerity.

But now, with Sassetta, we come on another aspect of the Middle Ages. Sassetta had neither the depth of religious feeling of Lorenzo Monaco, nor his attachment to Gothic line. What, above all, he took over from tradition was a desire clearly to bring out the thing portrayed and make it "typical"—which, in its naïve way, is a form of realism. And it was in this naïve intentness on things seen that he found an outlet both for his mysticism and for his poetic feeling.

In one of his greatest works, "The Mystical Marriage of St Francis with Poverty," all the ingredients of mediaeval taste are present in the simultaneous presentation of the Virtues meeting the Saint, and the Virtues ascending into heaven; in the Gothic line (which, however, is attenuated so as not to impair the plastic consistency of the forms), a line whose wave-like rhythm, extending from St Francis to the three Virtues in the sky, dominates the composition; and in the arrangement of the figures in the foreground so that the space behind, seen in perspective, has no more than a decorative value. Even that plastic realism, which he derived from those masters who had already embraced the ideal of the Renaissance, becomes, under Sassetta's brush, symbolic. In other words, though Sassetta had taken over some of the technical discoveries of Renaissance art, his outlook and ideals remained thoroughly mediaeval. What distinguishes him from his contemporaries is his craving for purity; and thus it is that, spurning earthbound reality, he sets his flight towards that ethereal plane on which every object becomes a lily, every line an arabesque, every colour translucent. Sassetta may have been a minor painter belonging to a school which, after its hour of glory in the XIVth century, had come to seem "provincial"—but this we must admire in him, that as an artist he was pure of heart.

Fra Angelico, however, was a very great painter, great also as a man most likely, and his art was far from simple. He owes his eminence to the tremendous vitality he gives his figures, even when they are personifications of the Christian ideal. The charm of his angels, his Madonnas and Saints has made him one of the world's best-loved painters. And this charm is but a touch of mother earth imparted to the denizens of heaven. His colour is not merely brilliant; it seems to glow with a celestial radiance, which nevertheless has something of the familiar light we know on earth.

Fra Angelico was an exceptionally pious man, a Dominican who favoured a reform of the Church, and a zealous opponent of the Franciscans whom, in his "Last Judgement," he consigns to hell.   After a period of recurrent struggles and exile, he became Prior of his convent, much beloved by a humanist Pope who him valued no less as a paragon of painters—the new Apelles—than as a faithful servant of God.   And without waiting for the Church to confirm his beatification, popular acclaim bestowed on him the name "Beato" (the Blessed).   Thus under these circumstances it is not surprising that he came to be regarded as the leader of the mystical school.

To-day, however, the mystical insight of such men as Berlinghieri, Cimabue, or Ambrogio Lorenzetti strikes us as being profounder than that of Fra Angelico; he ballasted his visions with too much real life for them to rise far above the mundane.   True, his work makes us feel that he is serving God, but also that he serves Him because he thus is serving the interests of his convent.   Duccio, we may recall, interposed the Church between God and himself; Fra Angelico interposes—his Order!   His simplicity is not that of a child opening his eyes on life, but that of a monk who has shut himself off from the world.

He studied in a school of illuminators, perhaps Lorenzo Monaco's.   Throughout his career he never lost his fondness for gold backgrounds, gracious lines, young and charming faces—all of which were fully in accord with the taste of late Gothic art. His knowledge of perspective was as thorough as Sassetta's, but he uses it for locating objects in Space, that is to say as the great Renaissance painters used it.   What is more, he had a quite exceptional ability for rendering plastic form.

Thus he endorsed the principles of Renaissance art, and turned them to account with prodigious skill and to the happiest effect.   None the less we feel that his ideal was not that of the Renaissance; he took over its methods with a view to enriching his technique, but departed from these whenever they seemed likely to endanger his personal, mediaeval vision of the world.   When, as occasionally happens, his vigilance relaxes and, in his admiration for the technical skill of the Renaissance, he allows its spirit to invade his compositions, we feel that their quality falls off.   The secret of Fra Angelico's undying renown lies in the pleasure all experience in seeing those sacred personages he portrays rendered exactly as the strictest theologian would have them be, and at the same time so companionably human.

LORENZO MONACO (1370 OR 1371-1425). MIRACLES OF ST BENEDICT. (11 ¾ × 25 ½") VATICAN, ROME.

LORENZO MONACO

During the last years of the XIVth and at the beginning of the XVth century, Florentine painting was at the cross-roads. Two tendencies were at work and both were gradually to lose in creative power. Even the contemporary writer Franco Sacchetti comments on " a sort of lassitude " that was coming over the art of his day.

Promoted by frequent contacts between France and Italy, Gothic taste was encouraging a refinement of line and of rhythm which might easily have led to pure calligraphy, had not Giotto's art still kept its old prestige. For the dawn of a new art, based on wholly new conceptions, Florence had to await the coming of Masaccio, as yet unborn. At the turn of the century painters, still faithful to the tradition of a Gothic art that had passed its prime, did not seek outlets for creative energy but chiefly aimed at refined, poetical interpretations of emotion.

Thus young Lorenzo Monaco, who came to Florence in 1391 with a view to assuming the white habit of a Camaldolite monk at the Monastery of Santa Maria degli Angeli, was involved in a period when the art world was torn by divided aims. Electing for traditional art, he applied himself to refining it and deepening its insight into the secret places of the heart. Of the various tendencies of the period it was those of Orcagna and Nardo di Cione that, generally speaking, he endorsed. They stood for a compromise between the plastic constructions of Giotto and the linear and colouristic innovations of the Sienese. And in the art of Lorenzo Monaco we see the culmination of the prevailing decorative propensities of Florentine art.

Born at Siena in 1370 or 1371, he devoted his whole life to the exercise of his two vocations, religious and artistic. He was appointed subdeacon in 1392, but becoming more and more absorbed in his activities as a painter, left the monastery in 1406 and in 1414 rented a house where he resided until his death, working with the collaboration of several pupils. The tenour of his life was unruffled by any striking event. Indeed he lived for his art, which he devoted whole-heartedly to the service of his faith.

The most famous works by this painter that have come down to us are the big polyptychs he made for the churches and convents of Tuscany, with their handsome predellas ; besides a good many pictures usually of the Madonna or the Crucifixion. He also did the frescos in the Bartolini Chapel at the Church of the Holy Trinity at Florence. Mention must also be made of his illuminated manuscripts, most of which are now in the Biblioteca Laurenziana at Florence.

Lorenzo Monaco's vast output has a remarkable homogeneity, which is due to that total harmony between the lyrical and mystical elements which meant so much to him, and in pursuit of which he kept to a treatment of lines and decorative colour that he worked out for himself. His painting, we feel, is the mature result of long and fruitful self-communings, and his style has some affinities with that of Ghiberti in the First Door of the Baptistery.

No less than by the tender emotion he imparts to the relationship between the Madonna and the Child, we are struck by his romantic feeling for landscape. In his later phase he moved towards a subtler rendering of the psychological aspects of his scenes, which is best illustrated in his small predellas depicting the life-stories of saints, in which the narrative is simplified and treated more broadly ; and to the recessional perspective poetically emotive values are now imparted. This applies also to the *Miracles of St Benedict*, now in the Vatican Pinacoteca. We are shown the saint resuscitating a lad who has been accidentally killed in the course of building a convent, while on the left a tiny devil is trying to lure away a monk during the service of Vespers.

With the peculiar rhythm imparted by the attitudes of the figures, the pallor of the tunics, and the rugged line of greenish rocks, the painter has created an almost spectral atmosphere, a world which, lacking any dramatic expression, seems haunted, nevertheless, by an awareness, tinged with regret, of the limitations its very ideal has imposed on it. Graceful, restlessly undulating, the Gothic line found an inspired interpreter in Lorenzo Monaco, who was destined to transmit his message to a host of minor painters, but to some great painters, as well—amongst them being Fra Angelico.

GENTILE DA FABRIANO

Gentile da Fabriano, who died in 1428 (date of his birth unknown), was a contemporary of Lorenzo Monaco ; but, while the art of both derived from Gothic, and both used line and colour for decorative effects (though, even in so doing, neither lost sight of the tradition of austerity bequeathed by early Florentine art), the two painters were utterly unlike. For each, after his kind, the mystic and the man who moved in court circles, while starting from the same premises, followed his own bent.

Born at Fabriano (a city of the Marches), as his name suggests, Gentile was the son of a highly cultivated man, a cloth-dealer by occupation and, incidentally, an astrologer. We know that in 1408 Gentile was in Venice where he had been asked to take a hand in decorating the Great Council Hall at the Ducal Palace. This is the first mention of him as an artist, but, from the fact of his being commissioned for this work, we may assume that his reputation as a painter stood very high already. Unfortunately these frescos perished in a fire (in 1577) which did much damage to the Palace.

Gentile spent his life moving from one Italian town to another to carry out orders given him by the greatest in the land. Malatesta called him to Brescia to paint some frescos for him and, while he was there, Pope Martin V, who happened to be visiting the city, asked him to come and paint at his court. Gentile, before he could get a safe-conduct and follow the Pope to Florence, had to give an assurance that he would not leave before he had finished his work at Brescia. Enrolled in 1422 in the Guild of Florentine Artists, he was authorized to open his own *bottega* there ; he gathered round him several assistants (amongst them probably being Jacopo Bellini), and made a hobby of collecting objects of art and jewellery of all kinds he kept in the courtyard of his " workshop." His work was greatly prized by the Florentines ; he was commissioned by the Strozzi family to paint his celebrated *Adoration of the Magi* (now in the Uffizi, Florence) and the fresco in Orvieto Cathedral ; these, apart from a few stray works dispersed in European and American art museums, are all that remains of this painter's considerable output.

In all his work we are conscious of that unique gift for harmony and grace which was brought to perfection in his maturity. The *Adoration of the Magi* may be regarded as the supreme masterpiece of decorative painting inspired by a spirit of " courtly " elegance. Not that religious feeling is excluded ; but here it manifests itself in a sensitive expression of blissful moments, the mood interpreted in those oft-quoted lines, "God's in his heaven, All's right with the world ! " Fanciful as is the depiction of the story, it blends harmoniously with the precision of the details, each of which is treated with loving care, and in which we see an almost oriental fondness for gleams of gold and precious fabrics, elaborate embroideries and decorative accessories spangling the scene with sudden glints of light and colour. The composition of the whole seems conditioned by these elements, and its poetic unity is ensured by an intricate, richly imaginative counterpoint of colours. The action spreads out across the three parts of the picture ; the motley retinue of the Magi—servants, astrologers, pages, palfreys, monkeys and the rest—converges on the centre of the picture, where we see the Three Kings themselves who, robed in garments glittering with gold, illustrate, in pursuance of an old tradition, the three ages of man. The detail on the extreme left—of the two servants—helps to emphasize the elegance of the group centering on the Virgin. In fact this picture marks the highest pitch of exquisite refinement which superb craftsmanship can attain in art. The gracefulness of the gestures, the soft luxuriance of silk and damask, the ivory sheen of flesh, beautifully contrived foreshortenings—all are bathed in a warm golden glow, the light, glimpsed by the poet, that never was on sea or land. And an adroit balance of line and colour holds all movement miraculously suspended in this brief rapture of a fleeting moment.

GENTILE DA FABRIANO (?-1428). ADORATION OF THE MAGI (DETAIL). UFFIZI, FLORENCE.

PISANELLO (1397-CA. 1450).   LIONELLO D'ESTE.   (11 × 7 ½″)
ACCADEMIA CARRARA, BERGAMO.

98

PISANELLO

Antonio Pisano, who, born at Pisa, came as a child to live at Verona, where he was nicknamed Pisanello, has one of the most attractive personalities in the long history of art. Throughout his work we find a poetic yet exact interpretation of visible reality, which, while recalling certain patterns of Gothic at its most luxuriant, has premonitions of the XVth-century Renaissance. This is due both to the composition and to the evocative power of his delineations. But what, above all, amazes and delights us in his art is his gift of expressing the fabulous and fantastic aspect of that remarkable period when the towns of Italy were ruled by great men who, murderous as were their habits, loved art with a great love ; when the courts were hotbeds of intrigue, but noble patrons aided artists by commissioning works which they were often hard put to it to pay for.

Of that spectacular age Pisanello's art is as it were a dream-picture, but one painted in full awareness that it is but the stuff of dreams. The artist tells his stories with a wealth of entertaining detail, embroiders on his themes, loads the backgrounds of his portraits with charming trifles, and shows us animals that seem to have stepped forth from some mediaeval fable. Thus in depicting the famous combat of St George and the Dragon, he freely infuses fantasy and poetry into the composition, in which we see horsemen, animals and the protagonists making ready as if for a joust-royal, while in the background of the picture two hanged men dangle on their ropes.

In fact all the work of this artist invites us into a world of fairy-tales and fantasy, in which however he never loses that feeling for realistic precision which his work as a graver of medals (of which he made a great many) had inculcated in him.

The dates inscribed on his medals throw light on the chronology of his career. But we also have fairly copious records of the life of this " *pictor egregius,* " supplemented by enthusiastic appreciations of his art in the literature of his time.

Like Gentile da Fabriano, Pisanello was a great traveller. We find him at Venice, when quite young, working on a fresco sequence begun by Gentile ; this, too, was destroyed in the 1577 fire. In 1422 he was at Mantua, and two years later at Verona, where the Gonzaga family gave him a monthly stipend and where, after an interval of two years in Rome, he settled down, as he hoped, for good. While at Verona, he kept in contact with the Estense Court at Ferrara, and made a present of two pictures to Lionello d'Este, one a *Madonna,* the other a *Julius Caesar.*

Towards the close of 1439 he took part in the abortive attempt made by Piccinino and Francesco Gonzaga to capture Verona. When the two commanders were constrained to retreat from the city, Pisanello accompanied them ; the penalty he paid for this miscalculation was that the Venetian government prohibited him from entering Mantua and Verona. Thereafter he lived under the aegis of the Court of Ferrara, where he painted the portrait of Lionello d'Este here reproduced. Ulisse d'Aleotti, the poet, tells us how the painter, after putting in six months' work on the portrait, " so as to give a true form to this figure, " found himself in competition with Jacopo Bellini, " *summo pittore,* " who had just come to Ferrara. It seems that Nicolo III, Lionello's father , was shocked by the somewhat harsh and rigid treatment of his model by Pisanello, as compared with the more indulgent methods of the Venetian. But Ludovico Carbone, a humanist who flourished in the second half of the XVth century, and owned this portrait, tells us that he could never look at it without being moved to tears, " so well had the painter brought out the intrinsically human side of his model. " The portrait is a highly successful work ; while clean-cut as on a medal, the features are softened nevertheless by the warm tones of the flesh and the green of the leafage in the background. With its discreetly restrained emotion, this composition has a noble, almost visionary quality ; minute as are the brush-strokes, there is a spacious warmth in the colour, and the whole seems radiant with an inner light.

In 1448 or 1449, the painter brought off a project he had long had in mind, of going to the Court of Aragon. At Naples he was kept busy on work of various kinds, ranging from the drawing up of plans for the arch of Castelnuovo to making designs for textiles and jewellery.

After 1450 we hear no more about him, and it may be assumed he died about this time.

It is a matter for regret that so few of his major works have come down to us. Amongst the little of his output that has survived are the decorations on the tomb of Niccola Brenzoni (San Fermo Church at Verona), an early work whose theme is an Annunciation, and the frescos illustrating the legend of St George in the Sant' Anastasia Church, also at Verona. The present state of the fresco at Ferrara (St Apollinaris) is such that we can form no satisfactory opinion of this work.

During the second period of his life, Pisanello painted many portraits, and several of these have survived ; also a few pictures dealing with religious subjects. Above all, he enjoyed vast renown as a maker of medals, and indeed some of those he made can justly rank as the most beautiful the world has known. Also a number of his drawings have been preserved, all of the greatest interest, especially the " Codice Vallardi " now at the Louvre.

SASSETTA

Sassetta was a second name given the artist Stefano di Giovanni ; he was thus named for the first time in 1752 (by a writer of the period), and since then the name has clung to him ; what it signifies is unknown. Indeed we know next to nothing about his life ; there is no reliable record of when or where he was born, though there are indications that Cortona, a small town in Tuscany, was his birthplace. But his true home, in the spiritual, perhaps also in the literal sense, was Siena. Not until 1428 did he enrol in the Guild of Sienese Painters, though five years before this the " Arte della Lana " had commissioned him to paint a large altarpiece, which may be regarded as his first " official " work. Three years later he was in touch with the Cathedral Chapter and working, along with others, on the famous Font, on which since 1417 had been engaged not only the Sienese Jacopo della Quercia but several Florentines, including Donatello and Ghiberti. It would seem that Sassetta furnished a plan for the architectural lay-out as a whole. Between 1437 and 1444 he made another altarpiece, this time for the Church of St Francis at Borgo San Sepolcro ; the scenes of *St Francis in Glory* on the front of this altarpiece and of St Francis' life (one the back) are now in London, Chantilly and the Berenson Collection.

In 1447 he was commissioned to make a fresco for the Porta Romana at Siena, but his death in 1450 prevented his finishing it ; this was left to another artist, Sano di Pietro whose work resembled his in many respects.

Art critics have taken different views regarding him. Mr Bernhard Berenson regards him as the greatest religious painter in Western art, and sees in his work the purest expression of the Franciscan spirit and a visual interpretation of the *Fioretti*. On the other hand the art-historian Mr Pope Hennessy does not find in him that Gothic grace which is usually ascribed to him, and holds that Sassetta comes nearer the spirit of the Renaissance, and sometimes displays a truly virile power.

Sassetta is, perhaps, too ingenuous, his soul too simple, for us to be justified in attributing to him the profound mystical vision of a man like St Francis whose preaching led all Christendom to take a new direction. Likewise his work, while showing leanings towards the new outlook which revolutionized Florentine painting in the XVth century, is still too hesitant, too remote from a full awareness of the great change that was coming over the world, for us to see in him a true Man of the Renaissance.

In his scenes of the life of St Francis, that of the *Marriage of St Francis with Poverty* achieves a lyrical beauty of a very high order with the radiance of its translucent sky, the rhythmical perspective of the landscape, and its naïve, almost " illusionist " rendering of each element of the scene.

SASSETTA (?-1450). MARRIAGE OF ST FRANCIS WITH POVERTY. PART OF THE ALTARPIECE OF S. FRANCESCO.
(37 ½ × 22¾ ″) MUSÉE CONDÉ, CHANTILLY.

FRA ANGELICO (1387-1455).   ANNUNCIATION.   MUSEO DI S. MARCO, FLORENCE.

FRA ANGELICO

Fra Giovanni da Fiesole, better known as Fra Angelico, is perhaps the most popular painter of the Italian Renaissance.   The blissful serenity of his religious pictures, his saints, " who seem more saintly than any others, " as Vasari justly said, and the limpid charm of his colours, make his work easily and delightfully accessible to the spectator.   Here are no clashes, no violent contrasts, no sophistications—it is like a paradise of painting before the Fall.

He owed that name " Angelico " so well becoming him, Vasari tells us, to the fact that " he never painted a Crucifixion without tears streaming down his cheeks, " and in the faces and attitudes of all his figures his tenderness of heart, his heartfelt faith in the Christian revelation, so visibly shone out.   And in fact his whole career was dedicated to his religious vocation ; he made it his life's task to body this forth in works of art.

Born in 1387 at Vicchio di Mugello, a village near Florence and not far from Giotto's birthplace, he entered the Dominican convent at Fiesole at the age of twenty, at the same time as his brother, who was a copyist of manuscripts.   This convent had been founded by

FRA ANGELICO (1387-1455). ANGEL MUSICIAN.
DETAIL FROM THE TABERNACLE OF THE LINAIUOLI ALTARPIECE.
MUSEO DI S. MARCO, FLORENCE.

Fra Giovanni Dominici, whose desire it was to restore to the Dominican Order the moral discipline of its early days. Young Angelico spent his novitiate at Cortona, returning to Fiesole in 1408. But the effects of the schism that had now developed in the Church made themselves felt even as far afield as Fiesole. Fra Giovanni Dominici disowned Alexander V, elected to the papacy at the Council of Pisa, and, having entered into conflict with the archbishopric of Florence, was obliged during the summer of 1409 to move his convent to Foligno where he had colleagues who shared his views.

The plague epidemic of 1414 forced the Dominicans to make another move, this time to Cortona. Only in 1418, when the schism had come to an end, could the brotherhood return to Fiesole. Fra Angelico was aged thirty-one at this time.

We know nothing of his work at this period ; nor, indeed, during the next fourteen years. In 1433 the " Arte dei Linaiuoli " commissioned him to paint a large altarpiece, which has survived and is one of his most famous works.

Like a frame studded with precious stones, a company of twelve angel musicians, in garments of jewel-like brilliance, surrounds the Madonna and Child. And in this work the ideals of mediaeval art and the dawning Renaissance find superb fulfilment. Are we to assume that his vocation as an artist came to Fra Angelico so late in life, in his forties ? This is hard to believe ; yet we have not the least evidence of any work done by him before this. At present art-historians are inclined to accept a theory, long controverted, that he began by painting miniatures. On this hypothesis, the shaping of Fra Angelico's genius would owe something to the School of Lorenzo Monaco, and it would explain his feeling for colour and the obvious delight he takes in it, as illustrated by his use of unmixed pigments, and his sensitive awareness of colour-relations.

FRA ANGELICO (1387-1455). DREAM OF HONORIUS III. FRAGMENT OF PREDELLA. LOUVRE, PARIS.

The *Annunciation* here reproduced belongs to one of four reliquaries made for the Church of Santa Maria Novella. There is much in it that calls to mind the technique of the illuminator : the minutely and lavishly decorated background, spread out like a carpet, the pink and blue patches of the small figures, showing up faintly in a haze of glimmering gold, and the sudden gleams along the folds of the garments. Though the exquisite grace of the angel, the Madonna and the bunch of flowers, whose value is so obviously linear, suggest an approach to the subject resembling that of Gentile da Fabriano in his *Adoration of the Magi*, there is a broadness in the drawing of the forms, and so much light is poured into the colour that we feel something more is present here than the spirit of late Gothic art—that we have already intimations of the Renaissance.

In 1436 Cosimo and Lorenzo de' Medici handed over the Church and Convent of S. Marco to the Dominicans of Fiesole, some of whom had before this been transferred to Florence. The convent was entirely renovated, and while the building operations were directed by the artist Michelozzo, Fra Angelico was entrusted with the interior decoration. He painted frescos in every cell, in every corridor ; these were not conditioned by the architectural lay-out of the building, but their places were assigned with reference to the religious rites and devotions taking place in the various parts of it. The inauguration of the convent took place early in 1442, in the presence of the Pope, Eugene V, and the work of the decorator won high approval.

Fra Angelico was one of the oldest of the first generation of XVth-century Florentine painters, being a contemporary of Donatello and only a few years younger than Brunelleschi and Ghiberti. There are many points of contact between the work of the last-named artist and that of the Dominican of Fiesole. In 1418, when Fra Angelico went to Florence, Ghiberti was at work on the first door of the Baptistery, and it was he who, in 1433, made the model for the Tabernacle of "l'Arte dei Linaiuoli." Thus it may well be that Fra Angelico acquired in part from him that splendid feeling for rhythm to which the lyrical charm of his composition owes so much ; also, perhaps, his special way of rendering perspective. Notable, too, in this connexion, is the new value given by Fra Angelico to the architectural elements. Thus, for example, in the Louvre predella, where in the dream of Pope Honorius III St Dominic is seen shoring up the tottering Church, the setting is a small square characteristically Quattrocento in its proportions, and the façade of the Basilica might have been designed by Brunelleschi. We find a vein of lyricism and fervent idealization pervading all that Fra Angelico set his hand to, and never did he deflect his art towards that somewhat analytic presentation, stressing new aspects of the human situation, which we find in Masaccio. What, most noticeably, these painters have in common is a tendency towards a geometrical simplification of forms. Nevertheless we know that Fra Angelico made a point of observing the new trends of art in his time ; indeed, according to Vasari, he did much towards shaping that long succession of painters who, " after studying Masaccio's frescos in the Brancacci Chapel, and exercising their 'prentice hands, attained to excellence."

The inauguration of the Convent of S. Marco brought, it seems, the painter into prominence, for the Pope invited him to Rome to paint the frescos in the S. Sacramento Chapel (no longer in existence). During his stay in Rome Fra Angelico undertook some work for the Cathedral of Orvieto, planning to carry it out in successive summers, but cut it short, owing, perhaps, to a tragic accident that befell one of his assistants.

After returning to Fiesole, where he was Prior of the Convent, Fra Angelico paid another visit to Rome, where he painted the frescos in the 'study' of Nicholas V, now called the Niccolina Chapel, at the Vatican. He died in Rome on March 13, 1455.

It was said that, to be able to paint angels so convincingly, Fra Angelico must have been used to seeing them around him. But it might also be said that he had the gift of transforming men into angels and saints, " making them so beautiful," as Vasari writes, " that they truly seem to be in Paradise." And in fact we often feel that his saints of both sexes are portraits — sketches from life, but charged with a power of transcendent evocation. His paintings might be described as visual commentaries on the Gospels, whose purpose is to interpret the highest ideals of the monastic life, and point the way to heaven.

FRA ANGELICO (1387-1455).   ST DOMINIC.   DETAIL OF CHRIST WITH THE SYMBOLS OF THE PASSION.   MUSEO DI S. MARCO, FLORENCE.

MASACCIO

While at the close of the Middle Ages men sought to find an issue from life's afflictions in dreaming strange, ecstatic dreams, in Florence, on the other hand, at the dawn of the Renaissance, men faced these afflictions and overcame them by constructive action, a remoulding of the "sorry scheme of things," and pride and courage were the order of the day.

But this venture was not to be undertaken light-heartedly; it called for discipline and planning. Moreover, the flights of mediaeval fancy had to be replaced by a sense of moral responsibility. Religion now meant more than the simple faith of the "Golden Legend"; it was based on ethical values, a christianized form of Stoicism. Thus we need not wonder if this change of heart led both to the Renaissance and to the Reformation.

There were three great pioneers of the new movement, men who, from early youth, entered heart and soul into the building of this new world: the architect Filippo Brunelleschi, the sculptor Donatello, the painter Masaccio. Brunelleschi, the eldest, is known to have been the inventor of the science of perspective, as used by painters. It is hard to-day to form a just estimate of the value of this invention, which enabled the artist to lay out his composition geometrically in Space before placing human figures in it. The immediate result was that with the aid of the new device the artist ascertained the correct proportions between men and nature and did away with the hierarchical proportions dear to the Middle Ages. Thus a new kind of unity was given the scene portrayed. We have already shown how in Duccio's art Time co-operates with Space in enabling the subject to unfurl itself across the painted surface and the observer to follow the sequence of events. But once the unity of Space was a "fait accompli," the artist could no longer narrate, he was bound to represent. Nevertheless the artists of the early days of the Renaissance felt it was incumbent on them to retain that "presentation" of the thing portrayed, which had been a basic principle of mediaeval art. Thus they sought, and found, a balance between "presentation" in this sense and the representation of Space.

Before the discovery of the "correct" proportions between man and nature, the figure had necessarily been the chief element in the composition. Now the invention of perspective tended to reduce the predominance of the human element vis-à-vis the immensity of nature. Nevertheless the XVth-century Florentines were far too proud of Man, lord of all things and centre of the universe, not to find some way of upholding his prestige in the painted scene. Their solution was to put him in the foreground and to lower the horizon line, thus giving an impression that, while situated in a perfectly normal environment, the human figure possessed a nobility, greatness and dynamism that lifted him on to an heroic plane.

But heroes are not mass-men; the artist had to render the hero as an individual and stress his physical vigour by the firmness of the contour lines—to adjust him, in short, to a statuesque ideal. By this means the artist could reconcile the dignified presence of the man of action with the geometrical requirements of proportion and perspective, and confer on his portrayal a stable, monumental majesty.

On the other hand, expression is a "movement" of the soul accompanying that of the body. Hence, in order to retain expressive power without losing this monumental value, it was needful somehow to impart the tension of movement to the static. Giotto had pointed the way to the solution of this problem, and the others followed in his steps. Thus we may say that the new way of seeing the world derived both from the application of perspective to visible reality and from a heightened mental and moral awareness. Religious faith acquired a new vitality, and that mystical surrender to the transcendental which characterized the earlier art, gave place to a concentration on the inner life of the individual. In fact it was not owing to any indifference towards religion but, on the contrary, to a new religious conception that the change came over art.

The gradual achievement of this Renaissance ideal of art was the life's work of Brunelleschi and of Donatello. As regards painting, this ideal found expression in the work of Masaccio, a revelation as sudden as it was compelling, and, brief as was his career (he died at the age of twenty-eight, after little more than six years' creative activity), its effect on art was lasting. Except for Brunelleschi, the discoverer of perspective, it would seem that he had no precursor.

It has been said that he took up painting anew at the point where Giotto had left it over sixty years before his birth, but apart from some temperamental affinities (impeccable taste and great creative energy), there is no real historical link between them. It has also, perhaps more justifiably, been said that he was a pupil of Masolino, with whom he worked at Rome and Florence. But that charming artist Masolino belongs to the tradition of the end of the Middle Ages, and the personal characteristics of Masaccio's art are diametrically opposed to the style of his elder and collaborator.

Thus it seems quite clear that Masaccio's creative genius, one of the most sublime the world has known, acquired from Brunelleschi's theory of perspective all that was needed—on the physical and even on the moral plane—to bring Renaissance painting, in one stride, to full maturity. Indeed his frescos in the Brancacci Chapel served as models and a source of instruction for several generations of painters, up to the XVIth century. And here we have another proof that the evolution of art is no uniform unbroken progress, but due to the sudden, unpredictable emergence of artists of individual genius.

Looking at works by Masaccio, we are immediately struck by the heroic quality he gives his figures, their monumental power and sovereign dignity. And we see, too, that by their volumes, no less than by their lay-out in depth, they build up their own Space. They do not copy nature; never have such heroes walked the earth. What we see here is an ideal nature so forcibly rendered that it seems not only real but typical as well. Each gesture is so telling that it seems inevitable, each is arrested at the moment of attaining its maximum intensity.

The Brancacci frescos are charged with high dramatic tension, but it is not released; it remains in the state of potential energy, an energy that seems inexhaustible—a source of heroic inspiration for all time.

In the "Crucifixion," however, the dramatic element is allowed full scope. Here, as in the Middle Ages, the painter used a gold background, but the plastic power given the figures by the strongly demarcated forms, the silent grief of the Mother in her dark cloak contrasting with the outstretched arms and red stridence of the Magdalen— all these are so completely detached from the background that its only function here is to intensify still more the colours.

Though in Masaccio's art these colours are in the Gothic tradition, they go beyond it and tend towards the conquest of natural light. Unfortunately we perceive this in some fragments only, so poor is the present condition of this work. Thus we cannot know how far the artist clad his compositions as a whole with this flooding light. Still this much we can say: that for Masaccio chiaroscuro was but a starting-point, never an end in itself.

The human element in Masaccio's art is homely, so to speak; the sublimity and heroism it attains is that of the plain man, who, like Christ, is of the people and has no pretensions to aristocracy. Indeed Masaccio could not be refined; he had too much to do by way of spade-work in founding a new culture. He has the rugged energy of giants and heroes; beauty in the ordinary sense he could not paint.

His beauty is the beauty of a rigorous synthesis, his form gives it its strength; and that is why he seems so near to us—the first begetter of modern art.

MASACCIO (1401-CA. 1429). CRUCIFIXION. (30 ¼ × 25″) PINACOTECA, NAPLES.

MASACCIO

That brief, spectacular incursion of Masaccio into the world of painting was an event as unpredictable as it was momentous. In a few crowded years, this painter, who died at twenty-eight, changed the whole face of art, and in him that age of intellectual ferment known as the Renaissance found a man capable of expressing in pictorial form its insatiable curiosity as to man and the world he lives in. Like a cataclysm he deflected violently the course of art from its age-old channels, and his contemporaries were no less conscious then than we are now, in retrospect, of the revolution he effected. Many were the artists who sought to learn from him the secrets of the methods he had discovered for expressing the new spirit that was active in the Italian world. Though actually older, Fra Angelico was the first of this series of "art pilgrims," which, including Raphael and Michelangelo, lasted on until the XVIth century. And even to-day, no lover of art but feels the mysterious grandeur of Masaccio's personality, and his amazing gift for penetrating to the very heart of human emotions. This was fully recognized in his own time and in the following centuries ; it was said that Masaccio was the first artist whose figures really had a footing on the solid earth. From the world that he created all merely decorative effects are excluded. Its denizens are peasants, and there is no question of beautifying faces ; humanity is depicted in its natural state, and these men and women are fully aware of their human condition, yet confident in their ability to hold their own in the scheme of things.

He was born at Florence in 1401, his real name being Tommaso Cassaio ; "Masaccio" was said to be a nickname, derived from "Tommaso" and implying "naughty Thomas." Vasari, however, will not hear of this derogative explanation ; how could a man whose good-heartedness was so patent have ever been thought "naughty"? Masaccio owed this appellation, he suggests, to the fact that he was always "up in the clouds, like somebody whose mind was so set on art and all concerning art that he gave little heed to himself and still less to others." Vasari adds that he had a supreme disregard for the practical concerns of life, even for his clothing, and often forgot to collect money that was owed him until forced to do so by sheer necessity. This is borne out by records that are extant, from which we learn that, even when he had plenty of commissions in hand, he was always heavily in debt, especially to the assistants in his *bottega*.

Nothing is known about his upbringing. When still quite young (on January 7, 1422), he enrolled in the "Guild of Physicians and Apothecaries" (which included the artists) at Florence, where he had already been living for some time. To this date may be ascribed his *Saint Anne, Madonna and Angels* at the Uffizi. This work is still in the traditional style, and it has recently been discovered that Masolino had a hand in it. This painter's name is often coupled with Masaccio's, not that there was any real affinity of temperament, though, as we know, these two artists often worked together. Nevertheless it was the elder of the two who underwent the influence of his junior, Masaccio.

One of the most important paintings on wood by this artist that has come down to us is a polyptych painted in 1426 for the Carmine Church at Pisa. It has been dispersed, some parts being lost, others having found their way to various art museums. The *Crucifixion* here reproduced is at Naples ; in it the artist's personal style is already fully manifest. The tautly circumscribed form of Christ, the fantastic elongation of the form of the Madonna, the agonized movement of the Magdalen's wildly outstretched arms, which finds a counterpoise as it were in the stability of the angles formed by Christ's arms—all these contrasting forms, "violently shattering the static balance," speak a language in which the tragedy is expressed in a plastic form at once controlled and charged with almost savage intensity. The colour may seem still to recall that of late Gothic, but the new "pure, unornamented form" (as a XVth-century writer described it) tells out strongly against the gold background —probably insisted on by the donor—owing to the play of the light which not only envelops the figures but brings them forward or moves them back.

MASACCIO (1401-CA. 1429).   BRANCACCI CHAPEL OF SANTA MARIA DEL CARMINE, FLORENCE.

MASACCIO (1401-CA. 1429).   ST PETER HEALING THE SICK WITH HIS SHADOW.   BRANCACCI CHAPEL,
SANTA MARIA DEL CARMINE, FLORENCE.

N THE BRANCACCI CHAPEL, SANTA MARIA DEL CARMINE, FLORENCE.

This sense of the dramatic is, perhaps, yet more pronounced in the frescos of the Brancacci Chapel at the Carmine, Florence, Masaccio's masterwork. Here he renders in a manner yet more impressive, yet more monumental, the powerful emotions quickened in him by his deep instinctual awareness of the destiny of man. Michele Brancacci, a silk-merchant, had been sent abroad on various diplomatic missions by the Republic of Florence. On his return, (probably in 1423) from a journey to Egypt which had involved him in considerable risks, he fulfilled a vow made in the hour of danger by commissioning Masaccio to decorate the chapel dedicated to "the Madonna of the People" in the Carmelite Church at Florence. Both Masolino and Masaccio were painters employed by the Carmelite ("Carmine") Convent; the former had been appointed in 1425 to carry out certain work in this church and Masaccio, too, if Vasari is to be believed, had already been employed on other work there.

The fresco sequence begins with two panels in the entrance showing Masaccio's *Adam and Eve cast out of Paradise* and Masolino's *Fall of Adam and Eve.* There used to be a continuation on the vault, but this has not survived, the vault having been repaired in the XVIIIth century. But copies of the frescos are available, and they show that Masaccio worked with Masolino from the start.

The two painters split up the work between them, according to their taste, without regard to continuity. Masolino had to stop work some time before 1427, when he went to Hungary as one of the retinue of "Pippo Spano," a distinguished soldier and King

1. Masolino. Fall of Adam and Eve.
2. Masolino. St Peter raising Tabitha from the Dead (Masaccio is thought to have painted the figure of the palsied man in this fresco; the houses and small background figures are also attributed to him).
3. Masolino. St Peter preaching.
4. Masolino. St Peter healing the man stricken with a palsy (*vide* No. 2).
5. **Masaccio.** St Peter baptizing.
6. **Masaccio. St Peter and St John distributing alms** (p. 117).
7. **Masaccio. St Peter healing the sick with his shadow** (p. 116).
8. **Masaccio.** Adam and Eve cast out of Paradise.
9. **Masaccio. The Tribute Money.** In three scenes (p. 115).
   1. Jesus and the Apostles arrested for failing to pay tribute. 2. Jesus tells St Peter to cast his line. 3. St Peter taking the piece of money from the fish's mouth.
10. **Masaccio.** St Peter invoking the Holy Spirit (repainted in part by Filippino Lippi).
11. Filippino Lippi. St Peter raising from the dead the son of the King of Antioch (thought to have been repainted by Lippi over a sketch by Masaccio).
12. Filippino Lippi. St Paul visiting St Peter in prison.
13. Filippino Lippi. St Peter delivered from prison by the angel.
14. Filippino Lippi. St Peter and St Paul before the proconsul.
15. Filippino Lippi. Martyrdom of St Peter.

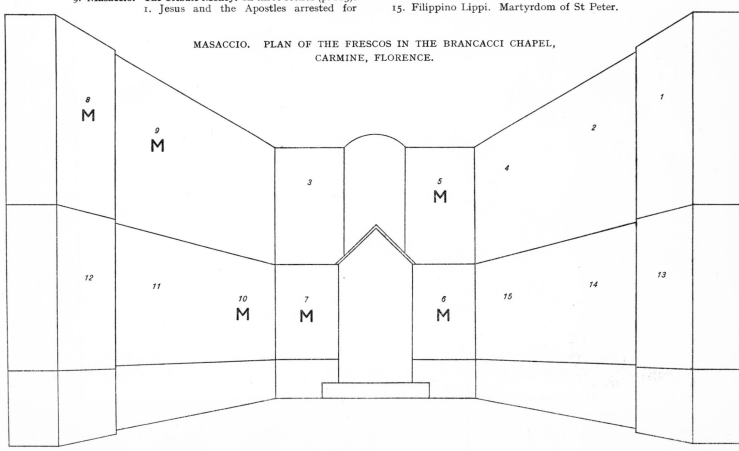

MASACCIO. PLAN OF THE FRESCOS IN THE BRANCACCI CHAPEL, CARMINE, FLORENCE.

MASACCIO (1401-CA. 1429). ST PETER AND ST JOHN DISTRIBUTING ALMS. BRANCACCI CHAPEL.
SANTA MARIA DEL CARMINE, FLORENCE.

MASACCIO (1401-CA. 1429). DETAIL FROM THE TRIBUTE MONEY. BRANCACCI CHAPEL,
SANTA MARIA DEL CARMINE, FLORENCE.

MASACCIO (1401–CA. 1429).   DETAIL FROM ST PETER AND ST JOHN DISTRIBUTING ALMS.   BRANCACCI CHAPEL,
SANTA MARIA DEL CARMINE, FLORENCE.

Sigismond's confidential agent. Thereafter Masaccio carried on single-handed, but he, too, had soon to abandon the work and go to Rome, where he died. The exact date of his death is unknown; all we know is that it took place between 1427 and 1429, most probably round about the latter date. The frescos made by Masaccio are relatively few in number; some fifty years later Filippino Lippi completed the decoration of the chapel.

One might almost say that this great work was dogged persistently by ill luck. Not merely does the number of artists who worked in this chapel make it very hard for the art-historian to feel sure of his attributions of the individual scenes, but the saltpetre in the plaster has injured some, and, crowning all, a fire took place which probably altered the colours. And, of course, there were the usual "restorations." (A plan is given showing the attributions now generally accepted.) But, despite these ambiguities and impediments, so great is Masaccio's art that it transmits his message across the ages; for, when all is said and done, his share of the work is readily distinguished, so eminent is its plastic and constructive power.

MASACCIO (1401-CA. 1429). DETAIL FROM ST PETER HEALING THE SICK WITH HIS SHADOW.
BRANCACCI CHAPEL, SANTA MARIA DEL CARMINE, FLORENCE.

MASACCIO (1401-CA. 1429). DETAIL FROM ST PETER AND ST JOHN DISTRIBUTING ALMS.
BRANCACCI CHAPEL, SANTA MARIA DEL CARMINE, FLORENCE.

PAOLO UCCELLO

FILIPPO LIPPI

DOMENICO VENEZIANO

PIERO

DELLA FRANCESCA

Masaccio is the complete artist; in his work form and colour, composition and expression, play their parts conjointly and combine to build up a perfect unity. In the whole history of art it would be difficult to find another painter so well balanced, despite the fervour of his creative impulse, and so sure of himself despite his youth and the revolutionary changes he was bringing to the climate of contemporary art.

Masaccio's "revolution" had prompt and stimulating effects in Florence. From the beginning of the XVth century up to 1450 and even later, Florentine architecture, sculpture and painting progressed from strength to strength, making this period one of the most brilliant and memorable in all art-history. Nevertheless, Masaccio's followers never achieved his perfect balance, and in making good their personalities, were inclined to press some of his tendencies to extremes. Nor did Paolo Uccello, Filippo Lippi or Domenico Veneziano break with the past so drastically as Masaccio.

Uccello's affinities with the Gothic tradition are evident both in the delicacy and choice of his colour schemes and in a propensity for those dream-like effects in which he gave free rein to his imagination. Only some four years older than Masaccio, he outlived him by forty-six. His influence made itself little felt, save on some painters of lesser stature, those, for example, who specialized in decorating "cassoni" (marriage coffers).

Uccello's early training was, it seems, on Gothic lines. It was his enthusiasm for perspective that led him to free himself from Gothic influences and made of him a true Renaissance—indeed a "modern"—artist. But his perspective differs from Masaccio's. Masaccio used the new discovery to implement a new conception of man and his place in the universe, whereas Uccello used it to escape from the world of men and roam at will in a realm of unbridled fantasy.

He made a fetish of perspective, practised it for its own sake, and learnt to render depth in a very striking manner; nevertheless he had a way of building up his compositions on the surface and, constantly shifting his angle of vision, of filling empty *spaces with foreshortenings which bore no relation to reality.   Moreover, those empty spaces were clearly meant to contain volumes, which Uccello was expert at rendering; yet, nothing if not capricious, he sometimes flattened out the figures or objects thus inserted, like shadows on a screen, so as to give the profiles more vitality.*

His colour is clearly of Gothic origin; yet, so as to realize more vividly his dream, he indulges in complementary contrasts or rather startling harmonies of colours.   With the former he secures light effects, always in the details, and not affecting the composition as a whole.   In his colour harmonies he uses pure pigments in a manner that is quite arbitrary as regards truth to nature; thus he does not hesitate to paint earth pink and human beings green, when this suits his purpose, with a mind to some purely imaginative pattern he has visualized.

The themes of such works of his as have come down to us lend themselves to fanciful interpretations of this sort: hunting scenes, battles, the legend of St George, that of the Jew and the Host.   In all these Uccello makes great play with perspective, pure colours, modelling; with profiles so wantonly exaggerated as to seem caricatures, and gestures odd to the point of phantasmagoria.   Likewise he indulges in such a number of foreshortenings in all directions, and in forms so abstract, that we seem to be looking at a mimic battle of marionettes rather than at real warfare. In Uccello's art reality and absurdity, facts and fancy, are interwoven in such a manner that he seems to anticipate some modern attempts to acclimatize, in art, the supernormal.

While Uccello's art is an expression of the unbridled imagination and, justly to appraise him, we should perhaps begin by endorsing the "near alliance" between genius and madness, that of Filippo Lippi is more normal in every way; its value derives from an innate sensuality held constantly in leash by the artist's reverence for his sacred figures.   As a man, Filippo Lippi was incapable of resisting the lusts of the flesh, but as a painter he is a monk conscious of his vocation; his art is edifying, though his life was not.

We may visualize a pupil of Masaccio who has learnt nothing of heroism but a great deal about the sensual value of plastic form.   Thus, in his art, form becomes lifelike, physically alluring; we can hardly decide whether we should admire it more for its convincingness and plastic solidity than for the exquisite delicacy and refined taste with which he renders it.   Nor must we overlook the earnestness with which he emphasizes the pious aspect of his art; and in this there is not the least hypocrisy, for, brush in hand, he is genuinely devout, contrite and sincere.

Masaccio's compositions are peopled by heroes, Uccello's by the denizens of some other planet, but Filippo Lippi shows us women who are agreeable to look upon, and attract us in a very human way.   Thus it was he who, taking over the heritage of Masaccio, gave it a wider appeal—popularized it, in fact—and stabilized it.

His colour schemes have a maturity ahead of his times; indeed in his art the last remnants of Gothic tradition are eliminated.   He realizes that his chiaroscuro, enabling those plastic effects he realized so magnificently, must absorb and limit his colour.   Though always delicate and delightful, his tints are not autumnal tints. With all his limitations Filippo Lippi is a poet through and through.   An unfailing sense of what is fitting, due to his moral instinct, bridles his sensuality at every critical moment. All he wants is to portray the life around him, with its pleasures of the senses, but likewise with its obedience to divine law.

Though born at Venice, in surroundings where the courtly influences of North Italian Gothic still prevailed, Domenico Veneziano, so far as his style is concerned, must be accounted a member of the Florentine school, such was his proficiency in perspective and the vigour of his drawing and plastic effects. We know very little about him; only that he claimed to rank beside Fra Angelico and Filippo Lippi. But one really great masterpiece by him has come down to us: the S. Lucia altarpiece, whose predella is dispersed in various art museums. And it explains convincingly why Veneziano's reputation stood so high.

Neither Angelico nor Lippi realized as well as he did the need for placing gaps between objects so as to situate them in space. And this use of the "caesura" creates a feeling of visual and mental repose, ensuring a happy balance of presentation and representation.

Obviously there was nothing of the dramatic in his temperament. Domenico was ravished by the beauty of the world and his vision of it was ecstatic. Under his brush everything takes on a new, supernal glamour, but quite otherwise than in Gothic art; for his beauty owes much more to a direct experience of reality.

At the origin of this ecstatic vision was coloured light. Masaccio had done no more than hint at the possibility of supplanting black-and-white chiaroscuro by purely chromatic values. And Angelico had sublimated his colours, giving them the smooth lustre of enamel-work or gems; though he came near the effect of natural light, he failed to bring it off. So far as we know, Domenico was the first to organize an entire composition in terms of coloured light and shade, thus creating the effect of the light of day. Nevertheless his shadows are hesitant and fall short of their full natural values; this, likewise, tends to make his tenuous, diaphanous light seem like a miracle of the imagination.

Thus a new unity of forms, colours and composition took rise with Domenico. He was shy of pressing his discoveries to their logical conclusion; that was left to his successors. But his work has the charm of the light of a summer dawn, a poetic touch of exquisite delicacy.

Modern criticism has given Piero della Francesca a place apart in the history of Italian art. And, in fact, his art seems at once a summing-up of all previous tendencies and a starting-point of all that was to follow, not in Florence only but throughout Italy. Yet, so vital is his personality that he seems rather to stand forth in solitary eminence, out of space and out of time. Though all the diverse elements of his style had been more or less foreshadowed, and were more or less inherited—their synthesis is his alone. And its secret died with him.

All artists who have attached a high importance to perspective derive from Masaccio. This is not the case with Piero; his attitude towards perspective is peculiar to himself. For Masaccio it was a window opening on a wider understanding of the world; for Uccello, a means of making his dreams come true. But Piero shared Plato's view that geometry alone is capable of imparting to form its absolute beauty, and in precise geometrical form he embodies both his supreme ideal and his experience of reality. As a scientist he writes about perspective and geometrical figures, but it is as an artist that he paints. For though he believes in mathematical formulae, he does not abide by them.

In his fresco at Arezzo, " The Visit of the Queen of Sheba," the point of sight of the perspective is set very low and thus the eye is free to roam over a vast recession, against which the figures in the foreground loom majestically, taller than life. Thus, progressing beyond the lifelikeness and balanced composition cherished by Masaccio, he indulges in a wider freedom, trenching indeed on fantasy.

For the presentation of figures in a scene, actual movement needs to be avoided. Giotto and Masaccio had made their presentations effectual by charging them with potentialities of movement that heightened their expressiveness. Piero, however, gives his figures such just poise and formal equilibrium that we do not feel them as being rigid but rather weighty and static, in the manner of a work of architecture. Thus his "monumentalism" is very different from Masaccio's; it is far less governed by actual visual experience. Likewise Piero displays amazing power in handling plastic form, which is more abstract and synthetic in his art than in Masaccio's. The latter got his plastic effects by ordinary chiaroscuro; Piero gets his by the use of colours, put on in zones, one colour representing light and the other shade. This was a wholly new conception; it is the basic principle of chromatic form in painting. With Piero light both surrounds and creates form, the effect being much ampler and richer than in Veneziano's art. All light vibrates, and natural light is fully rendered in painting only when free play is given to its vibrations, the dance of molecules. Piero's light, however, does not move; it illuminates and creates its own world, a world other than ours, august, serene, over which time flows unavailing, for it is founded in eternity.

Piero's style changed little if at all during his career; his earliest work shows him in full command of his powers. Nevertheless we perceive a more ideal beauty in the "Baptism," a work of his youth, than in the "Madonna and Angels," one of his last works; in the latter is more realism, a more concrete rendering of life. In the Arezzo frescos we may discern the perfect and assured balance of maturity. But it is a matter of shades of difference, hardly perceptible.

For all its unity and coherence, Piero's art is based on antitheses. Needless to say, every artist is, in the last analysis, both abstract and concrete; but Piero bodies forth simultaneously and to their maximum the abstract and the concrete—the former in his geometrical forms, the latter with an almost boundless realism. With Masaccio, for example, the claims of the structure of the composition are so pressing that he has no time to think of the arabesque; whereas, in Piero's art the two march side by side. In the work of many artists the monumental sublime ousts the beautiful; not so with Piero, whose work achieves an equilibrium so perfect between the plastic and poetic elements that it seems literally inspired.

At Florence, during the XVth century, more perhaps than in any other period, painters yoked art to science. Piero devoted himself to scientific research while none the less allowing his imagination the freest play; indeed in him the power of the imagination, creative of the truth, attained its apogee.

128

All the problems the Florentine Renaissance had set itself since the dawn of the century seem to have been solved by him; even, indeed, transcended, by grace of a special revelation granted to him alone.

At the same time Piero stands for a brief halt in art's advance towards the conquest of men and the world of things. He thirsted for eternity; therein lies his glory, but also his limitation, for life is more complex than contemplation of the eternal. And there were many other territories of the mind to explore before man and the world were conquered.

Piero della Francesca knew nothing of the tragic sense of life; his sublime heroes are too far removed from the human situation to suffer to the point of tragedy. Tragedy calls for movement, and, in art, movement, too, is a "motif" pertaining to man and nature, and above all to light, in virtue of its cosmic vibration.

There was no advancing beyond Piero on his path; after him art could but strike out in new directions. Indeed, already during his lifetime, new tendencies were coming to the fore in Florence.

PAOLO UCCELLO

A painting by Paolo Uccello, grouping, as in a frieze, a sequence of five portraits, in which the artist shows himself amongst those four men whom of all men he most admired, evokes more tellingly than words the tenor of this great painter's life. These four men are : Giotto, whose synthetic art impressed him above all ; then his contemporaries : his friend Donatello, Manetti the mathematician, and Brunelleschi the architect.

Paolo Doni, commonly known as Uccello, was born at Florence at the close of the XIVth century and his long life spanned the great period of the Renaissance. Like all his contemporaries he was much drawn to scientific research, and he was a keen student of mathematics, which appealed to him as fostering the maximum development of the mental powers of man on a pure, disinterested plane. But, no specialist, he was interested in all new discoveries. At the beginning of the century, thanks to Brunelleschi's architecture, the theory of perspective had acquired something of the grandiose simplicity of a mathematical problem set and solved, and Uccello was passionately interested in this subject. The story runs that one day he suddenly came out of a brown study, exclaiming : "Che dolce cosa è la perspettiva !"

On this count Paolo Uccello would seem typical of his age ; nevertheless his art did not altogether tally with the new ideal of the Renaissance. Rather he seems an artist born out of his due time ; his works have intimations of the old Gothic tradition no less than of the modern theories of the Cubists and Surrealists. Turning his back on the human and religious elements in Masaccio's art, he likewise paid no heed to the plastic problems which meant so much to his friend Donatello ; in a word, he does not seem to have shared in the enthusiasm of the men of the Renaissance for " the discovery of Man. " He was far more interested in animals, in birds especially (hence his nickname " Uccello "), in fairy-tales, and in the working out of mathematical proportions.

When barely ten years old Uccello was already working in Ghiberti's *bottega*, where his chief task was cleaning and " shining up " the Second Door of the Baptistery. At the age of twenty he enrolled in the Guild of Artists and in 1425 he moved to Venice, staying there for six years or thereabouts. We know little of his activities at Venice ; only that he took part in the restoration of the decorations at St Mark's and made, *inter alia*, a *St Peter* in mosaic (which has disappeared). We cannot doubt that he was affected by this contact with the world of Gothic art, then in its heyday at Venice.

In 1436, back again in Florence, he painted to order an equestrian picture of Giovanni Acuto, which he had to remake, as the committee concerned, who wanted an equestrian group looking like the translation of a bronze statue into terms of paint, disliked it. Vasari, too, disapproved of it, pointing out that the horse could not possibly have both right legs in the air at once, and failing to realize that this departure from reality was deliberate and imparted a special rhythm to the composition. The picture was signed " Uccello, " showing that he had already adopted this name " officially ." He was employed on various tasks by the Chapter of the Cathedral and was evidently prospering financially at this time, as he bought a house and land. His trip to Padua, on the invitation, Vasari tells us, of Donatello, probably took place soon after 1445 ; it would seem that during this visit he painted some giants, which subsequently were extolled by Mantegna, but we have no further information on the subject. Towards the close of his life he went to Urbino, where he painted his *Story of the Host*. On December 10, 1475, he died at Florence, probably in the public hospital, in utter destitution. Though Vasari misjudged the greatness of his art, he gives us a description of the man Uccello which, on the psychological side, is probably true enough. He describes him as " lonely, eccentric, morose and poor. Never giving himself a moment's breathing-space, he was always struggling to bring off the most difficult and impossible feats in art ; thus he was reduced to living in solitude, almost like a savage. "

Though Uccello lived almost to the age of 80, only a limited number of his works survive and we have, as usual, to deplore the ruined state of several of them. Thus

PAOLO UCCELLO (1397-1475). A HUNT. (25 ½ × 65″) OXFORD.

the fresco sequence of " The Story of Genesis" in the " Green Cloister" of S. Maria Novella (ca. 1431) is in a sad condition, and we have only tantalizing glimpses of the power these works must have displayed when they were new.

Three outstanding works of his remain to us, all on the same theme, *The Battle of San Romano.* They are to be seen in Florence, Paris and London, the London picture being the best preserved. Besides these we have the *Story of the Host,* in the Palace of Urbino, and the big hunting scene at Oxford.

Typical of the spirit of the Renaissance was Galileo's dictum : " The true book of philosophy, the book of nature, is writ in characters foreign to our alphabet. These characters are triangles, squares, circles, spheres, cones and pyramids, and other mathematical figures." This observation might almost serve as a description of the leading characteristics of Uccello's art. He was not interested in realistic portrayal, but in forms, and he studied these as such; while perspective gave him a wide field of investigation as to the relations of forms between themselves. But the strength of the artist lay in his ability for using his research-work as a means, not as an end in itself. Thus his treatment of perspective delights us, not as the skilful application of a system, but because the artist endowed it with a poetic content. In fact, Uccello had the gift of capturing the magical aspects of abstract forms.

Under the command of Nicola Maurucci di Tolentino the army of Florence won a great victory over the Sienese, and the rout of the defeated army inspired Uccello to paint the three battle-scenes entitled *La Rotta di San Romano,* for the ground-floor hall of the Medici Palace. The painter took such liberties with the historical realities of the battle-field that even in his own day the picture was jocularly called " The Tilting Match."

Each horse has, so to speak, a perspective of its own, independent of that of its neighbours, and thus acquires full individual value; nor is there spatial uniformity, or any great regard for three-dimensional volume. One might say that chief stress here is laid on the gaps between objects, the patterns hacked out by the arrested onrush of the horses, and those of the ground, which the débris strewing it cuts up into shapes having the constructive value

MANO.   (82 × 124¾″)   NATIONAL GALLERY, LONDON.

PAOLO UCCELLO (1397-1475).   THE BATTLE OF S. RO

Pl 62

PAOLO UCCELLO (1397-1475). STORY OF THE JEW AND THE HOST. FRAGMENT OF A PREDELLA. DUCAL PALACE, URBINO.

of solid objects. The lances on the left create an impression (which Giotto had already hinted at) of extreme rigidity and some grandiose geometrical design ; it is as if we were being shown a fantastic world of cataclysmic pauses, movements constantly arrested and resumed. The " action " of the battle does not unfold itself across the painted surface, yet it is not stationary ; it moves to a syncopated rhythm, with no ostensible coherence between details, yet with perfect inner coherence. All the terms of modern art come to our minds when we look at this picture : Cubism, broken rhythms and the like. Nevertheless this art is no mere display of brainwork ; Uccello has a natural gift for transmuting the fruits of thought into the stuff of poetry—a gift happily possessed by some of our modern artists.

Noteworthy, too, is the dream-like atmosphere of the *San Romano* battlepiece ; this derives from the light, which is not a specific, localized lighting any more than the colour is " local " or naturalistic. It is the light of the forms themselves, and we find this even more strongly present in *The Hunt* in which the red patches formed by the huntsmen and the yellowish streaks of the dogs seem charged with an impetus that will carry them forward to the world's end, and the light, neither of the day nor of the night, lends the scene the

other-worldly glamour of a fairy-tale.   Here, again (as also in the *Story of the Host)*, we find methods of expression remarkably like those of the most modern art.

In the predella now in the Museum of Urbino, which narrates the legend of the Profanation of the Host, we see another aspect of the dream-world Uccello had built up in his imagination.   This work may probably be dated 1467-68.   After this date Uccello became more and more absorbed in mathematical research-work, and gave little time to painting.

The small dimensions of the figure in the *Story of the Host*, and the pillars separating the panels might suggest that Uccello is harking back to the style of artists of an earlier age, the painters of the *cassoni* or wedding-coffers, which were generally embellished with figurines and ornamental subjects.   Actually in this work Uccello is once more breaking away from the Gothic decorative tradition, and his devotion to the abstractions of pure science has led him to plunge himself into a visionary world, in which, fantastic as they are, all the elements interlock with almost mathematical precision.   The architectural composition is skilfully devised with a view to giving the maximum value to the interplay of the lines, the figures in their somewhat stylized postures make us think of a puppet-show, and colour once again is treated not literally but as an abstract factor.

There is an eerie quality about these scenes ; indeed, even when we know the legend from which they derive, there remains an element of mystery.   Even the figures have attitudes of vague expectancy, as if waiting for some unpredictable event, or participating in some insubstantial pageant, the figment of a dream.

Uccello came in for some severe criticism from his contemporaries ; thus we are told that Donatello, friendly though he was, exclaimed, when invited to look at one of Uccello's pictures : " Really, you'd do better to hide it than to exhibit it like this ! "   And though to-day his is one of the great names of the Italian Renaissance, he is still regarded as something of an oddity.   Perhaps it is because, more than any other painter, he baffles us by the curious knack he has of weaving an esoteric poetry out of elements of mathematical aridity.

PAOLO UCCELLO (1397-1475).   STORY OF THE JEW AND THE HOST.   FRAGMENT OF A PREDELLA.   DUCAL PALACE, URBINO.

FILIPPO LIPPI

In studying XVth-century painting we discover that the word " Renaissance " conjures up a world so vast and varied that it is no surprise to find great differences between the painters of the period. Indeed, while making due allowance for tendencies which ran approximately parallel, it would be hard to find temperaments so unlike as those of gentle Fra Angelico and strenuous Masaccio, fantastical Uccello and sensual Filippo Lippi—to mention but a few of many similar instances.

Born around 1406 at Florence, Fra Filippo Lippi led an adventurous life. Possessing the true " artistic temperament, " he was at once impulsive, passionate and easy-going, and he combined much love of women with true devotion to religion. Having lost his parents in his early years, he was sent to a Carmelite convent at the age of eight and took vows when he was fifteen. There are records of his presence at the convent as late as 1432. A year previously he inscribed himself *dipintore* for the first time and it seems that in 1434 he accompanied his patron Cosimo de' Medici to Padua, where he did some paintings (of which no trace remains).

On his return to Florence, we find him, though orders for his work were frequent, describing himself (in a letter to Cosimo) as " one of the poorest of the brotherhood, " and asking for a loan of corn and wine " for his seven nieces. " Success came to him soon after, indeed he had almost more orders than he could cope with. When Fra Angelico declined to undertake the decoration of the cathedral at Prato, Lippi was next approached, perhaps on the initiative of Angelico himself.

In 1456, when about fifty, he was appointed to the Convent of Santa Margherita at Prato as Prior, and now began his romantic " affair " with a young nun whom he wished, at all costs, to have as his model for a picture. After much trouble he got permission to have her sit for him, the result being that he fell desperately in love with her, and ran away with her—and not only with her but with her sister and three others girls, her friends ! After the birth of his son Filippino (who also made a name for himself in art) Cosimo de' Medici persuaded the Pope not only to release the couple from their vows, but to solemnize their wedding.

Meanwhile, however, the work at the Prato Cathedral made little progress and the artist was frequently and forcibly enjoined to show more diligence. In 1464 the decoration was still unfinished ; this is the last information we have on the subject. In 1467 the painter began work on the frescos of the Spoleto Cathedral, and here too he was dilatory in his methods. At his death in October, 1469, much still remained to be done, and Fra Diamante, who for a long time had been assisting Filippo in this work, brought it rapidly to a conclusion. The frescos in the Prato Cathedral depict scenes from the lives of St John, St Stephen and the four Evangelists. What strikes us most from the stylistic point of view is the remarkable cohesion in this ensemble—so admirable indeed that art-critics are unanimous in regarding this set of frescos as one of Filippo Lippi's greatest works. Moreover there is good evidence that almost all of it is by the master's hand, very little having been left to his pupils. In the scene, *The Banquet of Herodias* here reproduced, the portrayal of the two girls whispering to each other has won much admiration. Here light is treated with much boldness ; the cream-white of the garments strikes a happy contrast with the white of the tablecloth, while their bright colours make the objects on the table and the tiled pavement tell out in the happiest manner.

We find in Lippi's artistic activities the same impulsiveness as that which made him notorious in his private life. He worked by fits and starts, as the mood of the moment took him. In his painting his qualities and defects as a man assume the form of a composition that often does not hold together, and a conception of space no more than approximative, but, it never lacks charm and gracefulness. His spontaneity, the freshness of his forms and colours and his inventiveness make his works particularly attractive. Indeed some of the *motifs* he was the first to introduce were taken up time and again by his successors. Thus we often see that woman walking with an airy, almost dancing step, her dress rippling in airborne folds around her form, and for many years to come painters sought to recapture

FILIPPO LIPPI (CA. 1406-1469). BANQUET OF HERODIAS (DETAIL). FRESCO, CATHEDRAL, PRATO.

the very human touch he imparts to the attitudes of the Madonna and Child in his religious art. The gesture of the Child stretching out his arms towards his Mother, surrounded by happy children who, mischievously smiling, seem to be casting glances at the spectator, points the way towards a rendering of emotions of a more familiar order, and, if on a less exalted plane than that of earlier art, having a more direct appeal. The portrayal of the Virgin still reigned supreme in all religious iconography, but such artists as Filippo Lippi were coming to express, through her, rather their joy in the beauty of women than a religious ideal.

DOMENICO VENEZIANO (?-1461). ALTARPIECE OF SANTA LUCIA. UFFIZI, FLORENCE.

DOMENICO VENEZIANO

In contrast to the complex and demanding art of Uccello, we find in Domenico Veneziano a model of the serene and easily accessible in painting, an adept of the light and graceful. His work, curiously worldly and pious at once, is indebted for its style to the most varied strains of his early-Renaissance contemporaries, and he shows leanings towards international Gothic, then still enjoying undiminished popularity among artists in northern Italy. Domenico was, as his second name suggests, a native of Venice. This Venetian origin (borne out by the fact that he signed his work *Domenicus de Veniciis*) may explain certain traits of his art, which, otherwise, belongs clearly to the new Florentine school.

The artist's date of birth is unknown. The first record we have of him is a letter to Piero de' Medici written from Perugia in 1438, in which he solicits a recommendation to Cosimo de' Medici and a commission for pictures. Domenico shows himself, even at this early stage, sure of his own competence as an artist, promising in his letter " to disclose to you things wonderful to see " and putting himself on a par with Filippo Lippi and Fra Angelico. This also implies that he was well versed in the Florentine painting of the time, and suggests he had lived there previously. All that we really know is that he did settle in Florence in 1439, remaining there until 1445. During these years he was chiefly engaged in decorating the Church of Sant' Egidio, assisted by, amongst others, Piero della Francesca. He died in 1461.

Beyond these few facts, we know next to nothing of Domenico's career. Many of his works mentioned by Vasari are to-day irretrievably lost. There remain, in fact, only two well-attested works by this artist, in addition to a few others whose attribution is uncertain.

The altarpiece for the Church of S. Lucia (now in the Uffizi) is one—and the more important—of these two. The figure of the Madonna, full of grace and vigour, faces us from amid her saints, grouped to the right and left, and in the diffused light mantling the other figures we have a foretaste of Piero della Francesca.

The altarpiece includes a predella, of which the *Saint John in the Desert*, here reproduced, originally formed part. With its synthetic rendering of the nude figure, its broad, grandiose treatment of the landscape and the luminosity of its clean-cut colours, this picture holds a very high place in XVth-century Italian art.

DOMENICO VENEZIANO (?-1461). ST JOHN IN THE DESERT. PART OF THE PREDELLA
OF SANTA LUCIA. NATIONAL GALLERY, WASHINGTON.

PIERO DELLA FRANCESCA

Though during the early years of the XVth century the plastic and dramatic art of Masaccio caused the Trecento art-world "to topple over like a card-castle" (as Longhi puts it), some years later the genius of Piero della Francesca, while brilliantly endorsing the newest tendencies of painting, revived traditions of the past. Some have claimed to discern in his work contacts with the art of ancient Greece and Egypt or even that of the Etruscans, but this seems rather fanciful ; what is more certain is that some aspects of his art derive from his immediate forerunners and contemporaries. Actually Piero's art is all-including ; at once grandiose and self-contained, it constitutes a universe in itself, something compact and self-complete — a world created by the artist. And if Piero's world is so acceptable to us to-day, this is not because its elements are combined according to laws with which we are familiar, but because, by the peculiar magic of his genius, it acts as an interpretation of our own world, that well might seem inscrutable but for the light thrown on it by some artists who are also "seers."

In the presentation of this world the artist assigns to each of his figures, to every landscape and each detail, the function of a piece of precise information to be added to the *ensemble* of his output, as if filling up a gap in it. Indeed Piero della Francesca's pictures are not to be considered piecemeal and independently, since each is a contribution to his creation as a whole, and implements it. Thus we find no "progress" from one of his pictures to the other ; this world he bodies forth has an organic unity, like that of a living creature governed by the laws of its own being.

The corrosive action of time has not greatly damaged his work, and has happily spared his biggest cycle of frescos, the decorations of the Choir of S. Francesco at Arezzo. Thus, though some of his works are lost, and others scattered in various towns of Italy and abroad, we have here a fairly complete conspectus of his output.

Little information is available as to his career, and nothing definite about his personality. Piero della Francesca was born some time between 1410 and 1420 at Borgo San Sepolcro, a small town near Arezzo. We learn that when quite young he was assistant to Domenico Veneziano, with whom he worked at Florence on the Sant' Egidio frescos (no longer in existence), but by 1442 he had already parted company with his master, for he was back again at his hometown. There he undertook to paint single-handed a polyptych representing *The Madonna of Mercy* within three years ; as a matter of fact he called in a Florentine painter to help him with this work, yet even so failed to deliver it on time.

The *Baptism*, now in the National Gallery, London, seems to have been painted during this period, but perhaps a little later than the Borgo San Sepolcro polyptych ; for it displays more fully the artist's personality. With its new treatment of bright light and especially by reason of the broadness of its composition, this picture imparts a feeling of profound inner repose and stability, giving it a place in that pictured "world" of Piero's to which we have alluded, and which was to find its full extension in the Arezzo frescos. All authorities on art concur in their admiration of this work—not merely for its superb treatment of the three figures of the angelic witnesses, but also for the detail of the winding stream mirroring the stately forms moving in the background, the white patch of the man who is making ready to be baptized after Christ, and the calm light that plays across the gentle slopes of the Tuscan hills in the distance. Indeed to-day art-lovers who visit this charming spot of earth see it through the eyes of Piero, as we see the South of France across the landscapes of Cézanne.

After painting *The Madonna of Mercy*, Piero visited Urbino, Rimini and Ferrara. It seems clear that quite early in his career he developed friendly contacts with the Court of Urbino. We have the evidence of Paccioli, the humanist, writing at the close of the XVth century, to this effect, and Piero della Francesca in his old age set it down in writing that he owed his renown entirely to the great kindness of Duke Federico, to whom, moreover,

PIERO DELLA FRANCESCA (BETWEEN 1410 AND 1420-1492). THE BAPTISM. (65 ½ × 45 ¼″) NATIONAL GALLERY, LONDON.

PIERO DELLA FRANCESCA (BETWEEN 1410 AND 1420-1492). FRAGMENT FROM THE STORY OF THE TRUE CROSS:
HEAD OF THE QUEEN OF SHEBA (DETAIL FROM THE QUEEN OF SHEBA WORSHIPPING THE WOOD OF THE CROSS).
FRESCO, CHURCH OF S. FRANCESCO, AREZZO

he dedicated his treatise on perspective, *De Prospectiva Pingendi*. His second treatise,
De Quinque Corporibus Regularibus, was dedicated to the son of Duke Guidobaldo. The
painter made several stays at the Court of Urbino in the course of his life, and painted the
famous portraits of the Duke and his wife, Battista Sforza. Seen in profile, in a sort of
diptych, husband and wife stand out against a landscape background stretching into the far

PIERO DELLA FRANCESCA (BETWEEN 1410 AND 1420-1492). THE BAPTISM. (65 ½ × 45 ¼ ″) NATIONAL GALLERY, LONDON.

S : THE QUEEN OF SHEBA WORSHIPPING THE WOOD OF THE CROSS.   FRESCO, CHURCH OF S. FRANCESCO, AREZZO.

PIERO DELLA FRANCESCA (BETWEEN 1410 AND 1420-1492). FRAGMENT FROM THE STORY OF THE TRUE CROS

PIERO DELLA FRANCESCA (BETWEEN 1410 AND 1420-1492). FRAGMENT FROM THE STORY OF THE TRUE CROSS:
HEAD OF THE QUEEN OF SHEBA (DETAIL FROM THE QUEEN OF SHEBA WORSHIPPING THE WOOD OF THE CROSS).
FRESCO, CHURCH OF S. FRANCESCO, AREZZO

he dedicated his treatise on perspective, *De Prospectiva Pingendi*. His second treatise, *De Quinque Corporibus Regularibus*, was dedicated to the son of Duke Guidobaldo. The painter made several stays at the Court of Urbino in the course of his life, and painted the famous portraits of the Duke and his wife, Battista Sforza. Seen in profile, in a sort of diptych, husband and wife stand out against a landscape background stretching into the far distance ; with his strongly marked features and stern expression the Duke seems to defy the world with proud aloofness.

While all trace of Piero's own work at Ferrara has vanished, there are indications of the great influence he exercised on the local artists.   His stay there, between 1448 and 1451,

PIERO DELLA FRANCESCA (BETWEEN 1410 AND 1420-1492).   FRAGMENT FROM THE STORY OF THE TRUE CROSS :
GROUP (DETAIL FROM THE QUEEN OF SHEBA WORSHIPPING THE WOOD OF THE CROSS).
FRESCO, CHURCH OF S. FRANCESCO, AREZZO.

coincided with one of the most brilliant periods of the history of Ferrara as an art-centre ; no sooner had Pisanello left, than Rogier van der Weyden and Mantegna (still in his boyhood) came to stay there. This, too, was the period when those great Ferrarese masters, Cosimo Tura and Francesco del Cossa, were taking their first steps in art.

At Rimini, in the Chapel of S. Francesco (built by Alberti), there is a fresco signed by Piero depicting Sigismondo Malatesta with his patron saint.

When he died, in 1452, Bicci di Lorenzo had not yet finished the painting he was engaged on in the Great Chapel of the Church of S. Francesco at Arezzo. Piero della Francesca took over the work (the exact date of this is not known) where his predecessor had left it and completed the figures of prophets in the vault above the entrance of the Chapel, whose walls he painted with scenes of the *Story of the True Cross*. Whereas, in the Brancacci Chapel of the Carmine Church at Florence, Masaccio had selected for depiction the most striking incidents recorded in the Gospels and the Acts of the Apostles, Piero embodied in his frescos a whole cycle of Christian mythology dear to the Trecento (Agnolo Gaddi, a pupil

PIERO DELLA FRANCESCA (BETWEEN 1410 AND 1420-1492). FRAGMENT FROM THE STORY OF THE TRUE CROSS :
THE ARMY OF THE EMPEROR CONSTANTINE. FRESCO, CHURCH OF S. FRANCESCO, AREZZO.

PIERO DELLA FRANCESCA (BETWEEN 1410 AND 1420-1492). FRAGMENT FROM THE STORY OF THE TRUE CROSS:
DETAIL FROM THE ARMY OF CONSTANTINE: THE TIBER. CHURCH OF S. FRANCESCO, AREZZO.

PIERO DELLA FRANCESCA (BETWEEN 1410 AND 1420-1492). FRAGMENT FROM THE STORY OF THE TRUE CROSS:
THE CITY OF JERUSALEM: DETAIL FROM THE FINDING OF THE CROSS. CHURCH OF S. FRANCESCO, AREZZO.

of Giotto had already used this theme in his frescos at S. Croce, Florence). Basing himself on the ' Gospel according to Nicodemus ' (as it figures in Voragine's *Golden Legend*), Piero narrated the story of the wood of which the Cross was made.

These frescos are arranged in a triple line, beginning with the topmost scene on the right, which depicts Adam in his old age sending his son Seth to the Angel guarding the entrance of Eden, to tell him how weary of life he (Adam) is. From the Garden Seth brings back a sprig plucked from the Tree of Good and Evil, which, on his return, he plants on the tomb (or in the mouth) of his father, who has died meanwhile. And from this branch grew the tree whose wood was employed for the making of the Cross. The legend is of epic length and Piero made a selection of its many episodes. The narrative proper begins on the second frieze where we see the Queen of Sheba refusing to cross a bridge made with the sacred wood, and kneeling in adoration of it.

On the wall facing the Choir we see Constantine's dream and vision, and, along the full length of the third row of frescos on the right-hand wall, the story of his victory over Maxentius. The victorious army is massed round the imperial standard. The central theme is the river whose smooth expanse has stayed the onrush of the massive warhorses, and, on the river's bank, the Emperor is holding before him, at arm's length, a small white cross. This cross stands forth, a clean-cut geometrical form, against the blue haze of the sky, while on the right we see the routed army which has vainly tried to cross the river.

In this fresco we have all the motifs building up the world of Piero della Francesca. That naked son of Adam whom we see from behind bringing the full weight of his body to bear upon his spade—an attitude at once statuesque and racy of the soil—is typical of all the other men Piero depicts, so firmly rooted to their mother-earth that one almost feels that, like trees, they are bred of it. Some have thought to see in these a reminiscence of Greek pier-statues, but their monumental dignity comes rather from the painter's instinctive feeling for the grandeur of nature and an inner visualization than from any deliberate recall. In *The Visit of the Queen of Sheba to King Solomon* the subject might well have given rise to a mere picturesque description of a gorgeous scene, but here, in the very sheen of the limpid colours, the monumental draperies, and the array of horses and human figures, we feel something utterly different from an anecdotal treatment of a legendary theme. The unfolding of the scene "by pauses," the tectonic concentration of the lines, and the abstract, architectural arrangement of the various elements combine in an effect of serenity so all-pervasive, a calm so profound, that we feel we are translated out of space and out of time, on to a plane high above the vicissitudes of the ephemeral, in which the words "eternal life" acquire their full and literal meaning. In short, this picture goes far beyond its legendary setting, and by grace of the artist's inner vision gives us access to a world apart, where no wind of change ruffles the peace of its perfection.

In *The Dream of Constantine* we have one of the first night-pieces in art. In his glimmering pallor the soldier seated outside the tent seems an effigy of frozen calm, luminous from within.

On the left-hand wall the narration of the legend pursues its course from scene to scene. Below we see in

PIERO DELLA FRANCESCA (BETWEEN 1410 AND 1420-1492). FRAGMENT FROM THE STORY OF THE TRUE CROSS. PEASANT : DETAIL FROM THE FINDING OF THE CROSS. CHURCH OF S. FRANCESCO, AREZZO.

PIERO DELLA FRANCESCA (BETWEEN 1410 AND 1420-1492). FRAGMENT FROM THE STORY OF THE TRUE CROSS.
SOLDIER : DETAIL FROM CONSTANTINE'S DREAM. CHURCH OF S. FRANCESCO, AREZZO.

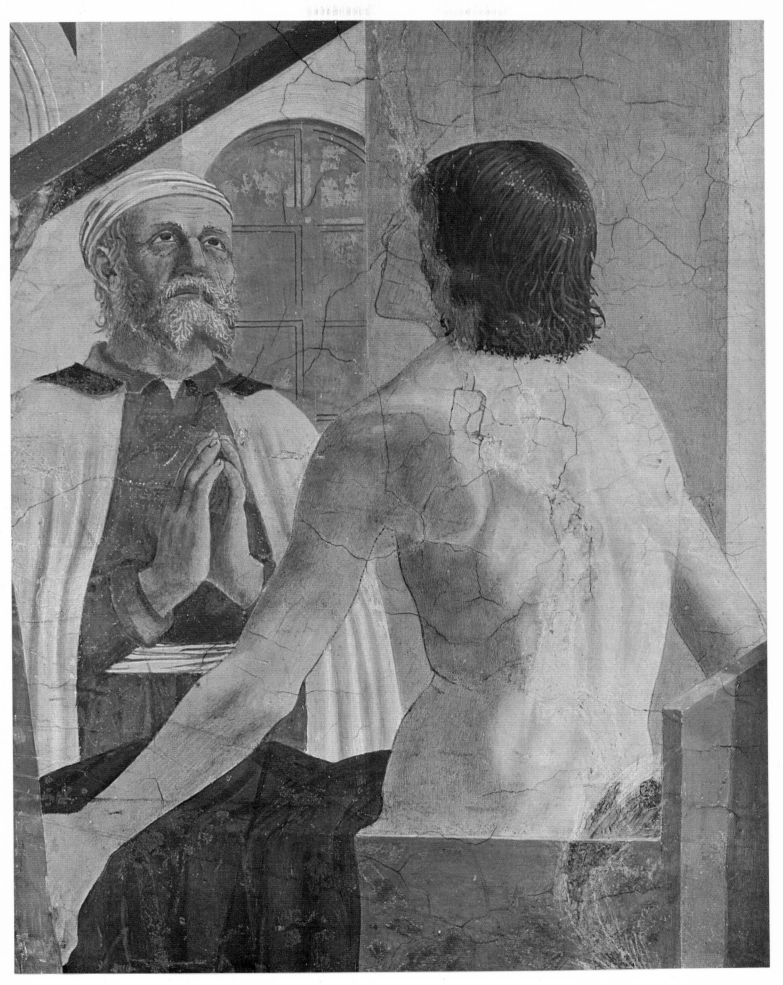

PIERO DELLA FRANCESCA (BETWEEN 1410 AND 1420-1492). FRAGMENT FROM THE STORY OF THE TRUE CROSS.
THE REVEALING OF THE CROSS. CHURCH OF S. FRANCESCO, AREZZO.

PIERO DELLA FRANCESCA (BETWEEN 1410 AND 1420-1492). MADONNA AND ANGELS. DUCAL PALACE, URBINO.

the *Defeat of Chosroes* a medley of faces, lances, and geometrical forms composed of broken glimpses of figures, limbs of men or animals; while, in contrast, the details in other frescos, treated with studied calm, have an amazing evocative power, independent of any "representative" portrayal. In the scene of Jerusalem, with its houses rising in tiers above the line formed by the horizontal beams of the crosses, we have a composition in which reality and imagination are marvellously blended. This is both Arezzo itself and the city of a dream. Similarly, in the adjoining group of grave-diggers (whose attitude recalls that of the 'son of Adam'), we see men who, while obviously peasants, are yet at the same time of high degree, men whose natural dignity is manifest both in their tranquil gestures and the calm glow of the colours.

It is clear that his contacts with the great artists of the previous generation and with his contemporaries contributed to the shaping of Piero della Francesca's genius. Though in early youth, at Borgo San Sepolcro, he familiarized himself with certain aspects of Sienese art, it was Florence that served as his true training-ground. In the study of perspective and in his geometrical research-work he saw portals of discovery which would enable him not only to view the world from a new angle but to find new explanations of that " classical " beauty whose almost scientific harmony was then the object of much attentive scrutiny. No doubt the young artist from Borgo San Sepolcro spent much time in the

PIERO DELLA FRANCESCA (BETWEEN 1410 AND 1420-1492).
MADONNA AND ANGELS (DETAIL). DUCAL PALACE, URBINO.

painters' studios, but he also saw much of L. B. Alberti, the architect and scientist, and learnt from him the theory of the Orders of architecture. And when we examine the rules on art laid down by Alberti, we have an impression that Piero must have studied them diligently, though he applied them in a different spirit.

While he is certainly to be regarded as a figurehead of the intellectual movement of the XVth century, the vitality of his colour, the stability of his forms and the "inwardness" of his expression rank him as one of the most sensitive and keenly imaginative artists that the world has seen.

Less mindful of the representation of nature and more profoundly imbued with religious feeling, Giotto attains a creative ecstasy which carries all before it; the art of Piero, on the other hand, is starker, more enigmatic, and perhaps the loss, if loss there be, in tragic emphasis is more than counterbalanced by that sense of the eternal immanent in all his art.

While painting the Arezzo frescos, Piero accepted other commissions. Thus in 1454 he undertook to paint within eight years, for a remuneration of 320 florins, a "Madonna enthroned with several saints." (Actually this picture was completed in 1469.) He seems to have gone to Rome during the period of the Arezzo frescos; in any case he is known to have been there in 1459, when he decorated with frescos those Stanze at the Vatican, which, later, Raphael painted; but his work there has not survived.

Between 1460 and 1470 Piero della Francesca was at Urbino and at Borgo San Sepolcro, where he undertook public functions, and thereafter he identified himself more closely with the civic life of his birthplace. We hear of his being, in 1482, Chief Prior of the "Confraternità della Misericordia." He also went to Rimini and settled there for a while; political troubles obliged him to leave.

The last years of his life were devoted to the study of perspective; at his death he left some treatises in manuscript, but these have disappeared. Very little is known about his declining years, probably because he developed cataract and lost his sight. He died in 1492; in his will he left instructions for his body to be interred in the family tomb at the Abbey of San Sepolcro.

ANDREA MANTEGNA
COSSA
COSIMO TURA

The new Renaissance style made its appearance in Northern Italy a generation later than at Florence, and its emergence was the direct result of work done on the spot by the great Tuscan artists: Paolo Uccello, Filippo Lippi, Piero della Francesca, Andrea del Castagno, and, above all, Donatello.

This circumstance that it was not an independent growth profoundly modified the character of the Renaissance in the North of Italy; Gothic tradition held its own much longer, and continued to make its influence felt in the spirit of the northern works of art. We cannot find in Masaccio a single element derived from classical antiquity; what is classical in his art, its grandeur, bears no relation to archaeological discoveries. In the art of Mantegna, however, particularly in the works of his youth, we feel that classical antiquity is his ideal. In the Eremitani frescos he deliberately portrays ancient monuments, Latin inscriptions, warriors in Roman garb, and a favourite theme of his is Caesar's triumph. As for his form, it looks like a transcription of Donatello's sculpture into terms of paint, with its incisive drawing, "illusionist" perspective, and Gothic colour so much modified by chiaroscuro as to be unrecognizable.

It cannot have been easy to weld together these diverse elements and therewith to build up an art ranking as a personal creation, but thanks to his genius Mantegna did so. There was much in him that was foreign to the life of his time, he had an excessive taste for rhetoric, and in his drawing there was pedantry and lack of ease—yet by the sheer driving force of his inspiration, the loftiness of his soul and strict self-discipline he transmutes these limitations into authentic art.

Mantegna's influence may be likened to that of Masaccio in central Italy; all the painting in Venice, Lombardy and Emilia during the latter half of the XVth century derives directly or indirectly from him.

That Ferrara, near Padua, had remained so mediaeval in its outlook, was due to the influence of the House of Este and their ideal of aristocratic elegance. Three painters of genius followed each other closely at Ferrara during the second half of the XVth century: Cosimo Tura, Francesco del Cossa and Ercole Roberti.

In all three we find clean-cut drawing combined with brilliant colour. What strikes us when we compare them with Mantegna is that they are much more interested in details than in the "ensemble," that they have no classical ideal, and that there is more vitality in their portrayals.

In Tura's "Pietà" (Venice) we have, in effect, Burgundian statuary set in front of a background which owes much to Mantegna; even the rocks are converted into spikes. The artist spares us nothing in the way of harrowing detail in his rendering of Christ's attitude and body, only the faces express a gentler grief. This work is highly original, the source of its power being the very unusual temperament of its creator, combining dynamism, even violence, with almost feminine sentimentality.

Francesco del Cossa has much in common with Tura, all whose qualities he possesses, with the addition of a more diffused light and a more sophisticated, if equally brilliant, colour. But he is not so deeply involved on the moral plane; he stresses lineal elegance and goes so far as to transpose St Lucia's eyes into grotesque flowers —an almost sadistic touch that Renaissance irony has forced on Gothic courtliness.

In their creative energy Tura and Cossa are men of the Renaissance, but the ingredients of their taste are still mediaeval. Their intriguing charm is due to this inner conflict of divided purposes, and they liberate themselves from Gothic art by stressing it to the point of paradox, and by satirizing its aristocratic propensities.

MANTEGNA (1431-1506). THE CRUCIFIXION. LOUVRE, PARIS.

MANTEGNA (1431-1506).   ST JOHN : DETAIL FROM THE CRUCIFIXION.   LOUVRE, PARIS.

ANDREA MANTEGNA

Mantegna's career as an artist extended over the whole of the second half of the XVth century. Born near Vicenza in 1431, he was the first North Italian Renaissance painter and his work is, in effect, a key to the understanding of the subsequent developments of the art of North Italy. In it he combines the new elements brought into art by the Tuscans with his native predilections, those of a man of the North born on Gothic soil.

While in the Florentine art tradition that vast movement known as the Renaissance had found a *terrain* fostering its development, things were very different in the North of Italy. There, by way of the Sienese and Burgundians, the Gothic art-forms had struck deep root, and likewise the gorgeousness of the East had made a strong impression ; thus the Northern temperament was ill adapted to promoting an art movement parallel to that of the Florentines.

Nevertheless, such cities as Venice, Padua and Ferrara, perceiving the excellence of the new art, commissioned Florentine artists for large-scale decorations. Though much was doubtless owed to the sculptor Donatello, we must also bear in mind that Piero della Francesca worked at Ferrara, Uccello lived seven years at Venice (whither Andrea del Castagno also came soon after), while Filippo Lippi spent six years at Padua and left a lasting imprint on Paduan art.

Andrea Mantegna was a precocious artist. When barely seventeen, jointly with Nicolo Pizzolo, he secured a contract from the Empress Ovetari who, in pursuance of the wishes of her dead husband, had a suite of frescos, narrating the lives of St James and St Christopher, made in the family chapel at the Eremitani Church at Padua. Three other painters were already employed on these decorations. Mantegna's share of the work, despite interruptions due to his travels, was completed in 1457, and constitutes the biggest *ensemble* made by the artist as a young man. Unhappily this fresco was destroyed in the recent war ; but it has been possible to reconstruct a few fragments.

In 1456, at Padua, Mantegna began a work commissioned for the Church of San Zeno at Verona ; four years later he completed it at the latter town. This altarpiece is one of his most celebrated works. While he was engaged on it the Marquis Ludovico Gonzaga several times invited him to come to his court at Mantua, and their correspondence, which has been preserved, has much interest. We learn that Mantegna could not accept this invitation in 1459 (though already he is named " familiaris " of the Court), but after 1460, though he made occasional trips to Rome and Florence, he was almost constantly with the Marquis.

His activities at Mantua were both varied and unflagging. With a staff of several assistants he made designs for tapestry, stage sets and dinner services, did portraits and engravings, collaborated in renovating the Palace, and painted in fresco the "Bridal Chamber," in decorating whose ceiling thanks to his expert craftsmanship and an amazing talent for perspective he carried " illusive painting " to its highest pitch, so that the figures seem to be actually floating in the air above us. Meanwhile he painted pictures for the churches of the city, indulged in constant quarrels with his collaborators and neighbours, and devoted much time to his collection of antiques.

The Marquis and his son Federico, who succeeded him, showed unfailing patience in their dealings with this touchy, self-opinionated and, above all, arrogant artist ; in recompense for his services they not only made him valuable gifts in money and in kind, but accorded him signal marks of favour befitting the sincere admiration they felt for his work. He died on September 13, 1506, of an apoplectic fit.

Mantegna's was a complex temperament ; he was much impressed by the new developments of art sponsored by the Tuscan Renaissance, and as enthusiastic as any Florentine over the new discoveries. Still it would seem that, coming later in the field, he flung himself with especial ardour into archaeological research, and the humanist enthusiasm of the Florentine artists took in his case a more literary turn ; thus, too, far more than they, he regarded the Renaissance as essentially a revival of classical antiquity. He had a passion for collecting ; a contemporary letter describes how in the company of the celebrated scholar Felice Feliciano he visited Lake Garda, in quest of epigraphs and antiquities. And when Lorenzo the Magnificent visited the painter in 1466 he was loud in admiration of his collection.

The *Crucifixion* at the Louvre originally formed part of the predella of the big San Zeno altarpiece at Verona. While in the large picture he applied himself to making a work strictly classical in its rhythms, spacious and objective in its treatment—one, in short, which would give scope for his brilliant craftsmanship—in the predellas, on the other hand, he allowed his imagination to range freely and indulged in the dramatic expression for which he had a natural gift. Thus the griefstricken apostle at the foot of the cross, the group of anguished figures supporting the Madonna, and the callous indifference of the group of dice-players—all alike affirm dramatically his tragic sense of life.

The *Pietà* now in the Brera Museum is justly famed for its happy combination of expressive power and accomplished craftsmanship. While maintaining the emotional tension, the painter has aimed at naturalism in his evocation of this oft-painted scene ; no longer focusing his interest on the human elements, he extends it to the whole face of nature, and his firm, clean-cut line is steeped in that all-pervasive chiaroscuro which, of all the artists of North Italy, Mantegna was the first to master. By reason of his ability to reconcile two tendencies which had long remained divergent, Mantegna stands for a turning-point in art, and for many generations his work was the lodestar of all commencing artists.

MANTEGNA (1431-1506). DEAD CHRIST. (32 × 27″) BRERA, MILAN.

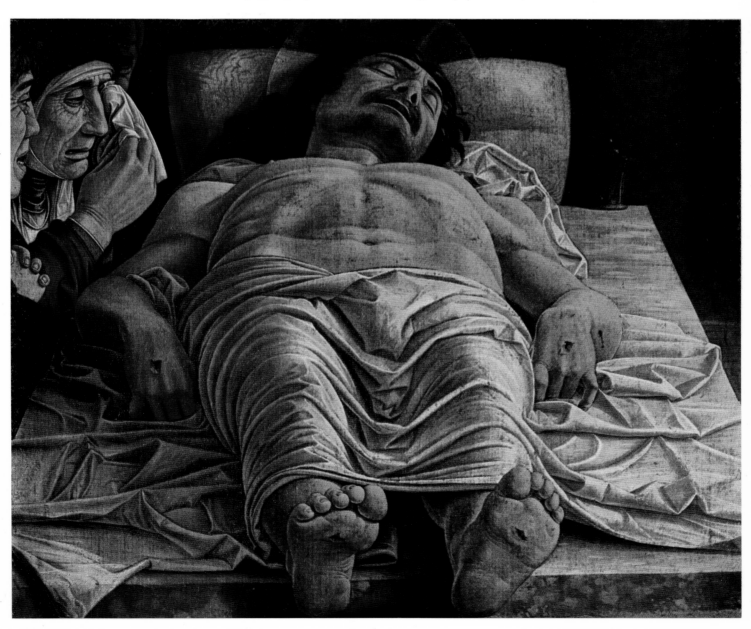

COSIMO TURA (1430-1495). PIETA. (19 × 13″) MUSEO CIVICO, VENICE.

TURA AND COSSA

As at Padua, Verona and Venice, it was during the second half of the XVth century that the Renaissance came to Ferrara, where three distinguished painters of the same generation —Cosimo Tura (1430-1495), Francesco del Cossa (ca. 1436-1478) and Ercole Roberti (ca. 1450-1496)—ushered in a period of high achievement in Ferrarese art. This famous town had been, and during the lives of these three painters continued to be, an active art centre and, as the works of Bellini, Pisanello and Rogier van der Weyden testify, Ferrara, like Padua, was in constant contact with Tuscan art. The presence of Piero della Francesca was a decisive factor in the new art movement. Yet, though there was much homogeneity as regards taste in Padua and Ferrara, the artistic "climates" differed considerably. At Ferrara the Gothic world was still a living reality. The feudal system and the age of chivalry held much of their old glamour, and while the Ferrarese delighted in all the beautiful things that enrich life, they likewise set much store by learning and the pleasures of the intellect. We have spoken of Mantegna's devotion to the classical past and to archaeological research, and in his case this was due to a very real spiritual need, for he had a scholarly and literary turn of mind. In Ferrara, however, the modish enthusiasm for antiquity became a stimulus to decorative effects, and somewhat " courtly " interpretations of the visible world, in which fantasy was allowed the utmost scope. Moreover, at Ferrara, the influence of Rogier van der Weyden superimposed on that of Piero and its formal rigour a keen interest in dramatic presentation.

Thus Tura and Cossa, like all those of their generation, were plunged into a period of conflicting tendencies. Indeed when we look into their work what strikes us most is the diversity of the elements that went to its making : a sophisticated Gothic, all in flowing arabesques, a desire for lifelike representation, and a quest of vigour and monumental structure.

Tura, who made his name as a painter when he was only twenty-one, was much sought after as a decorator. As well as doing murals in the d'Este Palace, he was responsible for the decorations of the spectacular pageants and tournaments organized by the Duke. One of his outstanding works is the painting on the organ-screen at the Ferrara Cathedral. Later, Duke Ercole, successor of Duke Borso, Tura's first patron, gave him commissions for a number of portraits.

Of Tura's enormous output as a decorator and portrait-painter but little has survived. All his frescos and portraits have disappeared. Thus for us his reputation must stand or fall by a very few works, enough however, to make us realize that his was one of the most singular and fascinating personalities of the Renaissance period in Northern Italy.

Francesco del Cossa was born at Ferrara some six years after Cosimo Tura . The first we hear of him as an artist is in 1456. While still quite young he had frequent contacts with Bologna, where he is known to have been in 1472, soon after he had finished the decorations of the Palazzo Schifanoia at Ferrara—a task for which he was very poorly paid, as we gather from a remark he made to Duke Borso. At Bologna he worked assiduously until his death in 1478, of the plague. During this time he made stained-glass windows for the Church of S. Giovanni in Monte, and painted the "Griffoni" polyptych, now regarded as the major work of his maturity, while the Schifanoia decorations illustrate his early phase.

The *Santa Lucia* here reproduced formed part of the altarpiece. The saint is holding her hagiological emblems, the palm-branch and the " bouquet " of her eyes—an allusion to the derivation of her name. As might be expected, we can trace in Cossa's work much the same influences as those in his contemporary, Tura's ; but it would seem that the art of Piero and that of the Florentines in general made a deeper impression on him. The light that floods the geometrically treated volumes of the Saint's face and the monumental effect of her form telling out against the gold background have a grandiose simplicity in which, however, we find traces of the ornamentation characteristic of late Gothic. Generally speaking, the impression produced by this work is one of a curious alliance of unexpected, indeed startling, elements with a formal balance of the utmost dignity.

FRANCESCO DEL COSSA (CA. 1436-1478). SANTA LUCIA. PHILADELPHIA.

ANTONELLO DA MESSINA
GIOVANNI BELLINI
CARPACCIO

The Gothic realism of Bruges and the geometrical ideals of the Florentine Renaissance were the loftiest forms of expression reached in painting during the first half of the Quattrocento. If it fell to Jan van Eyck to attain fine shades of luminous colour unrealized at Florence, it was none the less Masaccio, with other Florentine painters, who gave scope and unity to the space in which the figure was located. They it was, too, who first perceived the structural values of the figure, unknown as yet in Flanders. Yet, however divergent were the paths followed by the Flemings and the Florentines, the time soon came when they were led to pooling their respective discoveries. We may safely say that it was in Leonardo da Vinci, and in the XVIth-century painters in general, that the two tendencies finally coalesced in a definite and lasting manner. Piero della Francesca, as we have seen, took over certain Flemish devices, as did other artists of the Tuscan school. But the first fully to exploit a combination of Tuscan geometry and Flemish colour nuances was Antonello da Messina; and he effected the fusion of the two styles in works of the highest order.

That Antonello was able so successfully to assimilate the spirit and technique of a foreign art is in large part explained when we remember that many Flemish paintings, including those of van Eyck, were then to be seen at Naples. And it was there, according to a tradition handed down by Summonte, that Antonello was brought up by Colantonio.

His idealized, geometrical forms owe something to the influence of the Florentine painters, and that of Piero della Francesca in particular, though what actual contacts he had with them we cannot say. All we know for certain is that Antonello worked for the most part in Sicily and Calabria; in 1475, barely four years before his death, he came to Venice, and it was there that he first met with fame and recognition.

In his "Crucifixion" now at Antwerp, the twofold source of Antonello's style is clearly apparent. His colour has not the intensity and metallic sheen of Mantegna's, or of that of the Ferrarese painters. What was new in his painting was his treatment of nuances, the modifications of colour caused by light and bringing out the textures of objects. This procedure, typical of Flemish painting, is known as oil-technique, depending as it does on a much more expert handling of oil than any previously resorted to. Needless to say, this use of nuances to render the substance and texture of objects is a method eminently suited to realistic painting. We have only to compare, in this connexion, a landscape by Mantegna with one by Antonello and the difference is clear: the one abstract, standing on the expressive strength of its linework, the other concrete, sensitive and finely shaded, imbued with a simpler but more profound poetic feeling.

Antonello is indebted to the Flemish painters, not only for the quality of his colour, but also for a certain "intimacy" of expression, perhaps the best instance of which is the poignant visualization of the Virgin's grief in his "Crucifixion." This "intimate touch," moreover, accorded with Antonello's temperament: always concerned for the formal dignity of his style, he eschews all rhetoric whatsoever, even that of beauty.

His "Virgin Annunciate" at the Palermo Museum is characteristic of Antonello's geometrical conceptions. The use of a cone-and-cylinder lay-out to enclose the figure, the play of light emphasizing abstract forms, as in the book, the chin, the foreshortened right hand—all these confer an ideal quality on the figure, at once inscrutable and deeply impressive, of the Virgin. Likewise in the "Crucifixion" we may note his predilection for stressing the cylindrical form of trees and bodies. In Antonello's art we have a perfect synthesis between ideal, geometrical form and the realism of nuanced colour. The more his colour implements the particular, the more his form tends towards the universal.

During his lifetime, Antonello's fame rested above all on his portraits, and even to-day we seem to see in each of these the resuscitation of a real flesh-and-blood personality. Nevertheless we cannot fail to notice how the form of the eyes, for example, is abstract and geometrical in conception. And, paradoxically, it is just this form that we recognize as essentially true; almost one might say truer than reality.

Finally, apart from his creative mastery of form and colour, we feel in Antonello an objectivity, a capacity for seeing life steadily and whole—the outcome of his spiritual outlook on the world.

★

Precursor of the XVIth-century Venetian school, Giovanni Bellini was also the artist whose destiny it was to elevate Venetian painting to the level of that of Tuscany. He was the brother-in-law of Andrea Mantegna and son of Jacopo Bellini, who was esteemed the best artist in Venice between 1430 and 1450 and who gave a new form to Gothic tradition by grafting on it the elegant, if superficial, humanist culture of his day. His brother, Gentile, was a gifted artist in his own right, his fame extending even to Constantinople.

Thus in his family surroundings Giovanni Bellini became acquainted both with the canons of the best tradition and with the driving force of the best and boldest of the innovators. Thanks to an amazing power of assimilation he mastered both the Gothic tradition as reformed by his father, and the firm, constructive drawing of Mantegna. He clearly realized, however, that in the art of his father and brother-in-law mere craftsmanship (brilliant though it was) played too large a part. The *"finesse"* of the one and the dynamism of the other, while admirable in themselves, lacked somewhat in human warmth.

Giovanni Bellini was, above all, a poet, and a Christian poet—indeed one of the greatest of the Renaissance. All, to him, was the stuff of poetry, both delicate Gothic colour and the forceful line of humanist drawing; and he puts them to the service of his natural piety when he contemplates the Virgin and Child or the Passion of our Saviour. Thus, under his hand, both forms and colours are transmuted into the likeness of his secret vision; even his earliest works are masterpieces. The "Christ Blessing," now in the Louvre, is so intensely spiritualized that the borrowings from Mantegna implicit in its forms cease to be recognizable.

Similarly, in his "Agony in the Garden" (now in the National Gallery, London), perhaps intended to compete with Mantegna's version of the same theme (also in the National Gallery), we see how he has etherialized the heavy, earthbound forms of his model, and made his work a rendering of a sorrow transcending earthly grief. Mantegna's foreshortenings are, admittedly, more accurate; but Bellini felt he must do violence to the human material if he was to body forth the soul. He felt, yet more, that the divine figure should have in the very landscape an echo as it were of its spiritual anguish.

It may be that Bellini's reaction in terms of Christian piety against Mantegna's humanism was, in a sense, a "compensation" for the breach he was making with tradition. But his art was no mere psychological derivative. It corresponded to an overwhelming craving for reconciling knowledge and emotion, drawing and colour, man and the landscape, in a new synthesis.

Two things enabled Giovanni Bellini to draw away from the influence of Mantegna: his encounter with Antonello, his delicate colour and geometrical form, and his acquaintance with the work of Piero della Francesca (whether he actually met Piero we do not know). Some time prior to 1480 he took to forms whose continuity was based on planes rather than on lines, and a colour more responsive to varying degrees of illumination. Though a tone of Christian austerity still prevailed in his art, he gave more place to nature in her tranquil aspects, but a tranquillity always touched with gentle melancholy. The "Transfiguration" (at Naples) is very different from "The Agony in the Garden." Both are works of the highest order, and infused with the same poetic genius, but the later work shows a great change in treatment. In the "Transfiguration" the presence of the image is emphasized with far greater force, and in it the unity of all things, of heaven and earth, is effortlessly achieved.

After 1480, and until his death in 1516, Giovanni Bellini steadily perfected his style. In his later work he makes light penetrate more deeply into the texture of his pictures, handles nuances of colour more adroitly, and broadens his forms so that they respond more fully to their surroundings. More and more he bathes his landscapes in a heavenly light enveloping the world below like a benediction. Brooking no longer the handicaps imposed by his patrons, he lets his imagination soar on its own wings. And, without forgoing the austerity characteristic of his work, Bellini points the way to the romantic climate of Giorgione.

Giovanni Bellini contributed nobly and decisively both to the discovery of Man and the spiritual side of his nature, and to the revelation of the natural world and the soul immanent in all things. His early years belonged to the Middle Ages, and thus his activity as a Renaissance painter was of somewhat brief duration; but his last, triumphant phase linked up with modern art.

✶

Another highly gifted artist, closely related in spirit to Giovanni Bellini, gave the world a series of outstanding works towards the close of the XVth century: this was Vittore Carpaccio. His outlook was narrower than Bellini's and he devoted himself to painting the life of ease and luxury he saw around him. But he, too, was a poet, and there is an unforgettable charm in the directness, precision and, often, unexpectedness of the impressions he sets down. Having a limited ideal, he contented himself with these impressions and, while his handling of forms is in no way comparable to Bellini's, his colour is the gainer; a happy intuition guides him to enchanting harmonies of tones, put on boldly and without nuances. Carpaccio's "magnum opus" is the Saint Ursula sequence, at the Venice Academy. But his best known work remains "The Courtesans," that "slice of life" at once so quaint, so entertaining, and so delightfully modern.

In the above résumé we have somewhat neglected the art of Northern Italy: to name but a few of many, Paolo Veneziano, Vitale da Bologna, the Rimini artists, Tommaso da Modena, Giovanni da Milano, and Altichiero, all XIVth-century artists; Antonio Vivarini, Jacopo and Gentile Bellini, Ercole Roberti, Costa, Francia, Foppa, Bergognone, Montagna and Cima, who belonged to the XVth century. But it would have been impossible within the compass of the present volume to include colourplates illustrating the work of all these painters, excellent though they are.

Still a few words should be added regarding the climate of the art in Northern Italy at the close of the XVth century, when the effects of the Renaissance (deriving from Tuscany) were making themselves felt. In Lombardy Foppa had successfully combined Tuscan structural lay-out with the Flemish use of colour nuances, in a manner resembling that of Antonello da Messina, and thus prepared the ground for the new synthesis Leonardo brought to Lombardy, and which changed the whole contemporary attitude to art. And it was this synthesis that served Correggio as his starting-point at the beginning of the XVIth century.

Nevertheless, as is well known, Venice was the chief art centre of the North. And it is to Giovanni Bellini that we must look if we wish to understand that new, amazing development in painting associated with the names of Giorgione and Titian. The transition from Bellini's last works to Giorgione's early works is but slight as regards forms and colours; it is the spirit behind the works that has changed. Terms such as romanticism, pantheism, imaginative freedom, total independence of art as regards religion, may enable us to understand the new outlook on the world which both inspired the art of the best painters during three centuries and bridged the gap between the Renaissance and modern times.

ANTONELLO DA MESSINA (1430-1479).   VIRGIN ANNUNCIATE.   (13¾ × 13 ½ ")   PALERMO.

ANTONELLO DA MESSINA

In seeking to trace the origins of an artist of exceptional ability, we always come up against an element of the seemingly miraculous, and this is especially true of Antonello. Born at Messina (in 1430), Antonello took over, or invented for himself, the light which was a speciality of the Flemish painters, combining it with forms which bring to mind those of the Tuscan School. And thus he achieved a synthesis to which the Venetian painters of a later age continually aspired and which was, indeed, a ruling interest of the Cinquecento.

How was it that this Sicilian made acquaintance with these " international " tendencies? Vasari would have it that Antonello introduced the technique of painting in oils to Italy as a result of having travelled in the Low Countries and seen it in use there ; but this appears to be mere guess-work. The references to Antonello in the archives at Messina might suggest that though he was much appreciated as a painter, his fame was almost wholly local. Such, however, was by no means the case. His renown extended far beyond the shores of Sicily, and he was held in high repute, not only at Naples, but as far afield as Venice, Urbino and Milan. Indeed, when Antonello came to Venice, his influence brought about a transformation in the work of the greatest Venetian artists, and before long took effect on his contemporaries in Lombardy and Emilia.

Actually it would seem that his experiences at the Court of Naples did much to shape his genius. At that time Spanish culture and customs were greatly in vogue at Naples, and a number of Spanish artists painting in the Flemish tradition had settled there. We know that King Alfonso had a big collection of pictures at Naples, in which works by Jan van Eyck and Rogier van der Weyden had a prominent place, and also that Colantonio, Antonello's teacher, had thoroughly mastered the Flemish style. Such was the art climate of southern Italy at this time, and we may assume it was at Naples that Antonello first became acquainted with Tuscan art.

Our knowledge of his life is scanty. His father was by profession a sculptor, and his mother's name was Guarita. When he was about twenty-five, Antonello married and had two children. By 1457 he had evidently made his reputation at Messina, for in that year he received a commission to paint a banner for the Church of S. Michele. In 1460 he moved with his family to Calabria, settling at Amantea ; but we learn that he was back in Messina next year, and stayed there until 1465. This is the date on his *Salvator Mundi* (now in the National Gallery, London), the earliest work by Antonello known to us. No reference to the next eight years of his life exists. Then, in 1473, we find him again (or still) in Messina painting his polyptych, the *Madonna of the Rosary* (in the Messina Museum), and another church banner, no trace of which remains. Records for the year 1474 shows entries of payments made Antonello for various works, among them the *Annunciation*, now in the Syracuse Museum (Sicily).

In the following year he went to Venice and began work there on an altarpiece for the Church of S. Cassiano, some fragments of which are to-day in the Museo Civico, Venice. It was probably this work that brought Antonello's influence to bear most strongly on Venetian painting.

This year, 1475, made its mark in the history of Venetian art. For, with the coming of Antonello, Giovanni Bellini broke with the manner of his brother-in-law, Mantegna, and found new inspiration in Antonello's style. And Alvise Vivarini, then still drawing in a manner wholly derived from Bartolomeo Vivarini, now gave his art an entirely new direction, his example being subsequently followed by Cima di Conegliano, Bartolomeo Montagna and a whole new generation of painters at Venice and in Venetia.

Antonello himself, however, did not make an extended stay in Venice. We know that he was invited to the Court of Galeazzo Maria Sforza at Milan to paint various portraits, in 1476, but his stay was short ; before the year was out he was back at Messina. His death took

ANTONELLO DA MESSINA (1430-1479). BUST OF MAN. (11¾ × 9½″) GALLERIA BORGHESE, ROME.

ANTONELLO DA MESSINA (1430-1479). CRUCIFIXION. (23 ¼ × 16 ½″) MUSÉE ROYAL, ANTWERP.

place there on February 25, 1479 ; in his will he specified his place of burial and forbade his wife to remarry.

Such is all the records tell us of his career. But Antonello cuts so " international " a figure that we may well imagine he travelled far more widely than this. Also the information available regarding his personality is colourless and scanty. Thus we must turn to his works—unfortunately all too few are extant—if we wish to form an idea of the man he was. His pictures, many of which are dated, are scattered in art-museums in London, Paris, Vienna, Dresden, the United States and various Italian cities.

Though the influence of Flemish art is obvious in his early works, it is evident that, from the start, Antonello took liberties with van Eyck's technique, much as he was impressed by it, and used more continuous planes in an effort to give it greater compactness and unity. This new technique, though not endorsed by Rogier van der Weyden, reappears in the art of Conrad Witz and in the *Annunciation* at Aachen, at one time—probably wrongly—ascribed to Colantonio.

Between 1470 and 1475 his personal imprint becomes more marked, especially in the feeling for space apparent in his rendering of heads and in his cylindrical representation of the human form, pressed as far as visual reality permitted, just short of actual distortion. This latter tendency, so typical of his work, is particularly apparent in the Dresden *St Sebastian*, where the body of the saint is not merely supported by the pillar but actually forms one with it, thus producing an effect both unusual and impressive. It appears also in his portraits, where sharply defined zones of light and shade impart to forms a bizarre, magical suggestiveness.

We have already spoken of Antonello's great influence on Venetian painting. But it should be added that the influence was reciprocal, his stay in Venice having a deep and lasting effect on his art. The first work in which we perceive this is the portrait, *Il Condottiere*, in the Louvre (dated 1475). Here he is obviously striking out in a new direction, endeavouring in a general way to give a more vivacious expression to the face. After his return to Messina, the intensity of expression he sought to give his portraits centered on a glittering brightness of the eyes and a strongly affective line of the mouth.

Despite the relatively brief period known to us of Antonello's artistic career (no more than fourteen years) and the difficulty in assigning dates, we can " place " both the Antwerp *Crucifixion* and the bust in the Galleria Borghese as early works, while in the *Virgin Annunciate* in the Palermo Museum we find the artist's feeling for geometrical form carried to its logical conclusion.

GIOVANNI BELLINI (CA. 1430-1516).   LANDSCAPE : DETAIL FROM THE CORONATION OF THE VIRGIN.   MUSEO CIVICO, PESARO.

GIOVANNI BELLINI

Giovanni Bellini, son of the painter Jacopo Bellini, was born in Venice about 1430. Both Giovanni, an illegitimate son or the issue of a first marriage, and Gentile, his half-brother, made their names as artists.   But whereas Gentile produced works which, while showing some originality, are only of a relatively limited interest, Giovanni was the greatest Venetian artist of his day.   The two brothers often worked together, especially in their early years, and it is easy to see in Giovanni's work the influence of his surroundings in his youth.   Moreover, Mantegna married his sister ; thus it is not surprising that he was greatly influenced by Mantegna.

The first mention of Giovanni Bellini as a painter is dated 1460 ; in that year he produced a number of works, sometimes in collaboration with his father and brother.   Few of these have survived.

On August 28, 1479, the Venetian authorities decided to entrust Gentile with the restoration of the " Hall of the Great Council " at the Ducal Palace.   Owing to the dampness of the climate in Venice these frescos were not painted directly on the wall, the surface of which deteriorated rapidly, but on cloth.   Gentile, however, left for Constantinople and made over the work to his brother Giovanni, who spent thirteen years on it assisted by various artists, amongst them Alvise Vivarini.   But this work was totally destroyed in the fire at the Ducal Palace in 1577.

Meanwhile he made a number of cabinet pictures and some altarpieces now dispersed in art museums in various parts of the world; their themes are sometimes similar, but the artist brought to bear on each work a new poetic feeling giving it freshness and individuality. He also supplied pictures to many Venetian churches.

A series of letters that passed between Bellini and members of the House of Gonzaga between 1496 and 1506 have come down to us; full of small revealing touches, they throw much light on the temperament of the artist. On November 26, 1496, he informed the Marchesa Isabella Gonzaga, probably following up a previous conversation, that he would like to make a picture for her boudoir. In reply he was asked to paint a view of Paris, but Bellini declined, on the ground that he had never been to Paris. Which brings out the artist's desire always to express *direct* sensations. For this reply was certainly not due to any deficiency in his imaginative powers—he could have procured the necessary *data*, and starting from them made the picture —but to get the stimulus to paint, Bellini needed to be in direct touch with nature, with the light of his city, with places that he loved. His landscapes are neither heroic nor fantastic, they come from a direct response to nature, and a deep religious instinct leading him to include all God's works in his love of their Creator. Thus we can easily see why Bellini felt bound to decline the Marchesa's proposition; he could not undertake a "reconstruction" of the atmosphere of Paris, knowing nothing of its light or the colour of its buildings.

It was the Marchesa who six years later approached him, specifying the subject she had chosen. Bellini made difficulties; he said he was overburdened with work, would expect a lump sum in advance and a large allowance of time. Moreover he disliked the subject, fearing it would make him seem to compete with Mantegna. In fact Bellini kept putting the Marchesa off, always finding reasons for disapproval of the subjects she proposed, and this lasted until 1504, when the Marchesa, losing patience, asked him to refund the advances she had made. Whereat the painter promptly sent her the picture, apologizing for the delay, and explaining he was afraid the work might not be up to the standard she expected of him. Next year the Marchesa gave him another order, this time through an intermediary, whom the artist requested to tell her that "as to the treatment of the theme, this will be dictated

GIOVANNI BELLINI (CA. 1430-1516). AGONY IN THE GARDEN. (32 × 56")
NATIONAL GALLERY, LONDON.

by the imagination of the man who is painting the picture ; he does not like having his style cramped in the manner proposed, being used to taking his own line in his paintings." And indeed there could be little question of imposing the details of his theme on such an artist as Bellini. Though on occasion he could be humble, unsure both of himself and of others' approval, he insisted on absolute freedom of action where his emotional responses were involved. Here we have an attitude anticipating that of the modern artist.

Until the close of his long life Bellini held his place in the forefront of Venetian art. In 1507 he completed a work begun by Alvise Vivarini in the Hall of the Great Council, a work in which, in 1513, young Titian took a hand. On the death of his brother Gentile he took over the painting of a big canvas for the Scuola Grande di San Marco, but was unable to complete it. In 1514 he finished *Nymphs, Fauns and Musicians in Landscape* (now in the United States). "Very old but still the king of painters," Albrecht Dürer wrote of him in 1506, when at Venice. He died on November 29, 1516, aged almost ninety. In a contemporary diary is the entry : "We were apprised this morning of the death of Giovanni Bellini, that admirable painter, whose fame is worldwide ; for all his advanced age, he still was painting excellently."

Giovanni Bellini's career spanned the second half of the fifteenth century and the early years of the Cinquecento. Astride between two art-periods, he belonged temperamentally to the first, but pointed the way to the second, and indeed played an active part in it. Like his contemporaries, he realized that the old order was passing away, and there is more than a hint of melancholy in his art ; but his religious faith was too deeply ingrained for him to surmise that the world of Christendom he knew was tottering to its fall. Also he was a painter born, too fond of the radiant colours of the world around him and of the play of vagrant gleams upon the surfaces of things, not to impart to his portrayals of holy scenes, even the most tragic, something of his joy and trust in the beneficent care of God and nature.

Time and again he infused new life into his style. The altarpiece at SS. Giovanni e Paolo, the *Christ Blessing* at the Louvre, the *Agony in the Garden* in London, the Milan *Pietà* and the *S. Justina* in the Bagatti-Valsecchi Collection were obviously influenced by Mantegna. Indeed it was due to contact with his brother-in-law that he shared in the spirit of the Renaissance, though his temperament prevented him from indulging in Mantegna's excited handling of line. The Pesaro altarpiece (the *Coronation of the Virgin*) is the work which most clearly shows the new direction given him by the coming of Antonello, and his contacts with the forms and colours of Florentine Renaissance art. To this same period can be attributed, amongst other works, the Rimini *Dead Christ*, the Naples *Transfiguration*, the *Allegory* at Florence and the *St Francis* in the Frick Collection (New York). Towards the beginning of the new century, his young pupil Giorgione gave his master's art yet another trend ; for, old though he was, Bellini ever welcomed innovations opening new horizons. Thus now his feeling for nature grew more romantic, forms blend more softly in the chiaroscuro—in fact we have here, already, Cinquecento art. To this phase belong the *Madonna with St John the Baptist and a Female Saint* at the Venice Academy, the *Portrait of Doge Loredano* in London, the *Nymphs, Fauns and Musicians in Landscape* (U.S.A.).

Even when Bellini paints secular subjects, his handling of them strikes a religious note. But the subjects he most preferred were the Madonna and Child against a landscape background, and portrayals of Christ. On these themes he was capable of ringing the changes almost *ad infinitum*, in terms of variations in the landscape or the light, or of his responses to the poise of a head, a flash of memory or an uprush of emotion. But in the last analysis, many as were the influences affecting him—those of Mantegna, Antonello, Piero della Francesca, Giorgione—we find he took from them only the elements that suited him, and were indeed already implicit in himself. The dominants of his art were his love for nature and his mysticism which, intermingling, imbue it with intense poetic feeling ; thus in *The Agony in the Garden* the prayer arising from Christ's lips seems merging into the evening glow, and in the *Transfiguration* all nature joins in a paean of mystic exultation. And when this lyricism deepens into tragedy, the Mother and the Son seem, in their poignant grief, to be taking on their shoulders the burden of the sufferings of all mankind.

GIOVANNI BELLINI (CA. 1430-1516). CHRIST BLESSING. (23 × 17 ¼″) LOUVRE, PARIS.

GIOVANNI BELLINI (CA. 1430-1516). LANDSCAPE: DETAIL FROM THE MADONNA AND CHILD WITH ST JOHN THE
BAPTIST AND A FEMALE SAINT. ACADEMY, VENICE.

VITTORE CARPACCIO

Born in Venice about 1455 of old Venetian stock, Vittore Carpaccio likewise ended his life in his native city. Despite certain Eastern motifs in some details of his pictures and the inevitable influence of his contemporaries and predecessors, he found in the colourful life of Venice his inspiration, and his work maintains throughout an unmistakably Venetian accent.

The earliest written mention we have of Carpaccio is a Will (dated 1472) made in his favour by Fra Ilario Zuan Carpaccio.

Until recently the general opinion was that Carpaccio studied under that indifferent painter Bastiani, but modern art-historians have reverted to an earlier view: that he owed much to the teachings of Gentile Bellini (Giovanni's brother). And in view of the frequent contacts which we know to have existed between Carpaccio and the Bellinis in executing various works of art they were engaged on, we may well assume that he was their pupil as well as their collaborator. The distinctively narrative style of his art reminds us of that of Gentile, who likewise shared Carpaccio's fondness for depicting the city and its life under all its various aspects. Gentile's lively scenes, his marvellous skill as a colourist, especially in rendering the lustre of rich materials and the sudden gleams that play on water, are paralleled by the virtuosity displayed by Carpaccio in narrating the legends so popular with the public of his day. But Gentile's art shows some affectations, and his scenes do not always come to life as happily as do Carpaccio's. In fact Carpaccio's treatment of his subjects is at once freer and more coherent ; also he puts more poetry into it, and a more loving care for details. Mr Bernhard Berenson has aptly pointed out that in the work of Gentile, Cima del Conegliano and Carpaccio, we have as it were a reflection of the vivid and colourful life of their time. Festivals of all kinds were the order of the day ; and vast sums of money were expended in making them as elaborate and spectacular as possible. Thus, too, speaking of Renaissance Venice, Miss Helen Gardner writes : " A fervid patriotism made strong demands upon its citizens for the glorification of the state. There were gorgeous pageants and ceremonies, both religious and civil, besides private banquets and pompous balls, the richest costumes of stiff brocades, gold embroidery, and lavish lace and jewels. "

Carpaccio's earliest extant work is a nine-part cycle painted for the Scuola di S. Ursula between 1490 and 1498. From panel to panel, the artist narrates the legend of Ursula, the maiden whose hand the son of the English king had sought in marriage—showing, among other scenes, her farewell to her parents, the annunciation of her martyrdom, her entombment and her apotheosis. From the first panel (done in 1490) onwards, we are able to follow the evolution of Carpaccio's style. Thus, the scene of Ursula's dream is all in muted, softly vibrant undertones ; then as the panels succeed one another, the treatment of the pictures grows more animated, the air brighter, and the flooding light brings out the almost oriental splendour of this world of fairy-tale, rendered with such delightful realism by the artist. Thus we see, in the *Reception of the Ambassadors*, the figures moving with freer, ampler gestures ; and now we realize that the heart of the tale beats in the sultry air of Venice, the shimmering radiance of the lagoon, which bathes the whole composition in a sheen of colour no artist before Carpaccio had attained.

Between 1496 and 1500, Carpaccio, in collaboration with Gentile Bellini and other artists, was working, for the Scuola di San Giovanni l'Evangelista, on the "Miracle of the True Cross." Generally speaking, he did not trouble to centralize the leading motif in the picture, but indulged a taste for freer narrative. Also he loved to present his tale in settings drawn from the brilliant life of Venice as he knew it. He takes delight in "illusionist" perspective, the glittering play of light on water, and builds up a three-dimensional space in which each figure moves to an individual rhythm.

Naturally these new anecdotal methods, based on the scenes of daily Venetian life, rule out the expression of any deep religious feeling. For, despite his contacts with Giovanni Bellini, his elder, Carpaccio's bent was not towards a mystical interpretation of the

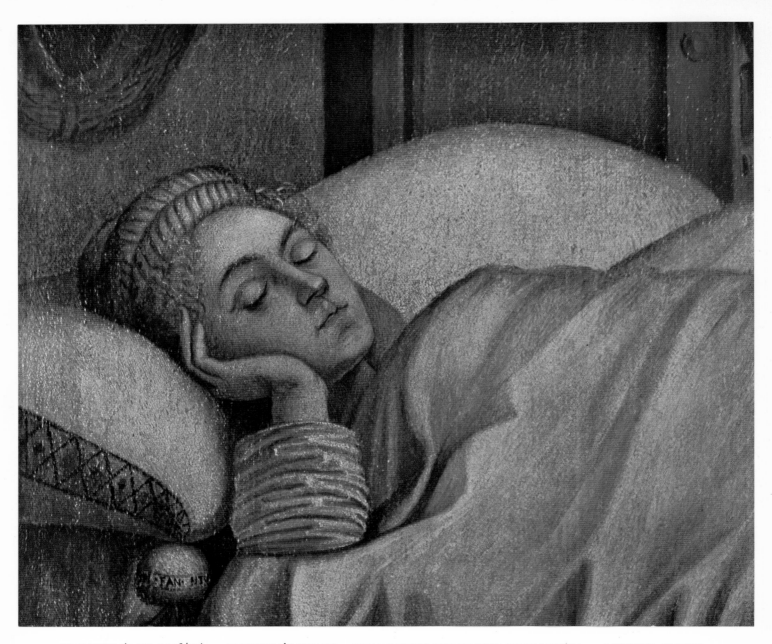

CARPACCIO (1455-1526/27).　ST URSULA'S DREAM.　DETAIL FROM THE LEGEND OF ST URSULA.　ACADEMY, VENICE.

visible world.　In fact his gift for rendering brilliant light effects and his exceedingly skilful drawing almost make of him a " genre-painter. "　If, from the whole of his output, there remained to us no more than his altarpieces, the esteem in which we hold him would be seriously diminished, the value of his colour notwithstanding.　Even when he seems, deeply and reverently, to feel the agony of Christ—as in the great picture at the Metropolitan Museum in New York—he cannot, it seems, control his taste for the romantically macabre.　This is much in evidence in the landscape serving as background to the fight between St George and the Dragon, figuring in a cycle painted for the Scuola di S. Giorgio degli Schiavoni, where among some of his finest achievements, are to be found others of a much inferior order.　The freedom of movement imparted to the figures of St George and the monster is such that the very ground beneath them appears to be dropping away.　The dragon and the horse together form a long decorative line streaming across the picture, while St George seems chiefly intent on the gesture he is making, one of the utmost elegance.

St Jerome in his Study, belonging to the same period, is a delightful work, full of inventiveness and fantasy ; the light and shade seem playing hide-and-seek with each other, while the details of the room are stated with whimsical precision.

His cycle for the Scuola di Santo Stefano dates from the period 1511-1520, while his paintings for the Ducal Palace were destroyed in the fire of 1577.　Records in Venice for the year 1508 include Carpaccio in a committee of artists called on to judge the murals done by Giorgione for the " Fondaco dei Tedeschi. "　His death took place in 1526 or 1527.

We have in Carpaccio neither an innovator nor a reformer. In an age of intense scientific curiosity, when artists were enthusiastically following up new lines of research, he seems to stand apart, unable to turn his eyes from the city he loved, and loved to paint, so that others too might perceive her beauty. The clear, limpid light of Venice, the variations of colour in aerial perspective—these are the leading themes of his art, and in treating them he displays a sensitive response to light effects and a freedom of execution (depending far less on the drawing than on tonal harmonies) which go far to explain the highly personal charm of this great Venetian's work.

CARPACCIO (1455-1526/27). ST URSULA TAKING LEAVE OF HER PARENTS.
DETAIL FROM THE LEGEND OF ST URSULA. ACADEMY, VENICE.

CARPACCIO (1455-1526/27).   TWO COURTESANS.   (64¾ × 37″)   MUSEO CIVICO, VENICE.

ANDREA DEL CASTAGNO

POLLAIUOLO

ANDREA VERROCCHIO

SANDRO BOTTICELLI

Neither Uccello nor Filippo Lippi, neither Veneziano nor Piero della Francesca had a sense of the dramatic. Yet, as we all know, drama plays an essential part in human life and often makes its presence felt. Florentine painting in the XVth century certainly could not ignore it, considering the social and moral conditions of life in Florence during the second half of the century, when there were only too many incentives to dramatic representation.

Andrea del Castagno came down from his mountain home, endowed with all the rugged vigour of the hillman, and tried his 'prentice hand at painting hanged men. He was gifted with an extraordinary power of assimilation. Masaccio's drawing and plastic form, Piero's light and colour, had no secrets for him. But nothing in them was strong or violent enough for his liking. So he turned to Donatello, whose sculpture revealed a driving force akin to his own. His figures are giants who, one feels, should be always engaged in fighting; even when, in his art, they are not thus engaged, their bodies lunge forward in a fierce display of energy.

Nevertheless when his theme is suffering humanity, Christ's passion or his death, then we see these "giants" suffering—and terribly! In these works Castagno's deep spiritual feeling is plain to see. His plastic power implements the expression of physical agony, while his luminous colour conveys the most delicate nuances of mental anguish.

Andrea del Castagno, who died young, in 1457, bequeathed to Florence and Venice a new, poetic rendering of grief and an example of unflinching courage in exploring the abysses of the soul.

Yet it was not Castagno who gave the new spirit stirring in Florence its essential form, but Antonio Pollaiuolo, who founded a new school of painting. A fact that Lorenzo the Magnificent recognized when he said: "Antonio is the supreme master of Florence, perhaps there has never been a better painter."

His art is characterized by three directives: movement, accentuated line, anatomy.

Though it was recognized that emotions of the soul are made manifest by movements of the body, Florentine art tradition, as exemplified in Giotto and Masaccio, *elected to portray the visible world and particularly the human form, stilled, as it were, in ecstasy; the reason being that dignity and monumental grandeur are incompatible with movement. Thus the expression of emotion took the form of a tension, a potentiality of movement rather than actual movement. Piero della Francesca pressed this ideal to its extreme limit; indeed the emotive power of his figures comes from their very immobility. Pollaiuolo was still too respectful of tradition to interpret movement literally, as activity; what he did was to give his figures postures in terms of movement—which, to his mind, was a legitimate form of expression in art, since thus the artist was treating dynamism as a human attribute, and not indulging in a mere "illusionist" device.*

There are various ways in which this kind of movement can be rendered, and Pollaiuolo's was by means of line. By dint of breaks and contrasts, his contours thrust their way into bodies, agitate them and launch them into space. During the period extending from Masaccio to Piero, line had ceased to take the lead in painting; modelling had replaced it, and artists paid more heed to bodies themselves than to their linear contours. Whereas Masaccio created movement by volumes, Pollaiuolo indicates it by his line; moreover he loved line for its own sake, for the vitality and beauty implicit in it.

When, ceasing to be expressed by volumes, the human form is rendered in terms of contour, details and likewise the focal points and interrelations of the different parts of the body stand out more clearly. Obviously this calls for a careful study of the structure of the body. Pollaiuolo knew all about anatomy, and the display of it he makes in his paintings and engravings proves his interest in it. It was owing to him that Florentine painting, in which during the first half of the century perspective played so large a part, was characterized in the second by its interest in anatomy.

Pollaiuolo did much in shaping the taste of his age; apart from his dynamic line and the vividness of his delineations, there is a vibrant quality in his art which we cannot fail to notice. He is conscious of the vitality immanent in all things, everywhere. While in the "Rape of Dejanira" in the Jarves Collection the human forms suggest movement by their attitudes, a vibrancy is imparted to the surface of the river by brushstrokes of a kind that owes nothing to the plastic traditions of the time. And here we see the work of a creative genius in advance of its age and opening new horizons.

Having, like Pollaiuolo, begun with sculpture, Andrea Verrocchio was similarly interested in contours and anatomy. But he was a much sedater artist, not at all a "world-shaker." Anxious above all to "make a good job of it," he concentrated on his craftsmanship, which was of a high order, and on effects of plastic relief, while his imagination had a relatively narrow range. Thus, as an artist, he was well qualified to discover what could suitably be taken over from Pollaiuolo's more daring flights of fancy, with a view to adjusting it to the taste of the times. While greatly daring artists are usually most admired, the more cautious artist who keeps his feet firmly planted on mother earth gets more orders. Thus, though Pollaiuolo's art was loudly acclaimed, it was to Verrocchio that the authorities of Florence and Venice turned when giving orders for works of art, particularly sculpture.

He was Leonardo's teacher; indeed, Leonardo owed to him the grounding in art which prepared the way for his triumphal progress.

Verrocchio's greatest painting is undoubtedly the "Baptism of Christ," in which Leonardo painted the angel on the left and probably the patch of landscape above the two angels. As contrasted with the solidity and forthright craftsmanship of Verrocchio's share of the work, the complexity and subtlety of Leonardo's is already manifest. Nevertheless this does not diminish our admiration for the plastic qualities of the figures of Christ and the Baptist, the power and sense of human dignity the artist has imparted to them ...

Before passing on to Leonardo da Vinci we must speak of Botticelli. A pupil of Filippo Lippi, he also took over some methods from Pollaiuolo, Andrea del Castagno and Verrocchio. He mastered all his predecessors had to teach him in the way of perspective, anatomy, construction of the human form, and rendering of movement. Nevertheless he employed what he had thus acquired in reverse, so to speak; perhaps because his art coincided with the beginning of the crisis of Florentine culture at the end of the XVth century. This crisis was of a moral order; faith in man and his omnipotence was failing, and desperate efforts were being made to cling to the "old-world" transcendent values, belief in which was ceasing to be possible. In these circumstances Botticelli's attitude was one in accordance with his naïve and sensual temperament; he took life as it came, keeping to a precarious course between the pagan propensities of the Medicis, his patrons, and the gloomy apostrophes of Savonarola—like a cork bobbing on the eddies of a troubled stream. Botticelli had not the spirit of a reformer as regards either his religion or his life; he merely sighed—and in that delicate nostalgia consists the peculiar charm of his art.

For many centuries after his death his greatness was unrecognized; it was left to be rediscovered in England between 1867 and 1871. Walter Pater was keenly alive to the fascination of this artist, all of whose figures are "in a certain sense like angels, but with a sense of displacement or loss about them—the wistfulness of exiles, conscious of a passion and energy greater than any known issue of them explains, which runs through all his varied work with a sentiment of ineffable melancholy." Thus Pater and his followers saw above all the "decadent" side of Botticelli, his languorous femininity, and a morbid sensibility finding its best expression in his angels.

All this, doubtless, is present in Botticelli; but there is something more. And it was this "something" that caused the change in our estimate of this artist which occurred at the turn of the century, the starting-off point being an observation made by one of Botticelli's contemporaries: "His works have a virile look, are excellently ordered and perfectly proportioned." Here, then, we have him in a new light; besides the qualities Pater found in him, there were others, as, agreeing with the contemporary opinion cited above, we now recognize. In fact there was much boldness and virility in Botticelli's art, and behind it lay very great technical competence and a thorough understanding of perspective. Also, his painting has plastic relief, realistic objectivity, moral force and (contrary to the Botticelli "legend") a broad, monumental style.

He is not one of these "conquerors of man and nature" whom we associate with the Renaissance; indeed he seems to hark back to the Middle Ages and the Gothic style.

Yet this is only in appearance; the power of his expression makes the dream he bodies forth more real than reality. His art has both a feminine and a virile side; in it melancholy tenderness and manly forthrightness are wedded, blend together and become one, in the same way as form and content are at one in a successful work of art.

When we compare the Three Graces in " Primavera " with his Saint Augustine, we see two aspects of Botticelli's personality, of his creative unity and his greatness as an artist. As for " La Derelitta," it is the work of a genius who, leaving behind the methods of all Schools and theories of art, has taken wing into the realm of the purest poetry and the eternal human. Here all is an exquisite awareness of the frailty of woman, infinite compassion for a loneliness that hides itself from the world, and indignation with that door for ever closed against all human charity.

Ruskin was first to observe that Botticelli's attention is focussed on contour lines. In this preference for lines as against volumes and colours lies his limitation; but it lies also at the root of his power and his supreme achievement. Much as he studied and admired Pollaiuolo's line, he put his own to a different use; he conjures up in his mind's eye strange arabesques and rhythms, like those of some slow, gently swaying dance— lines which are grace incarnate and bestow grace on all they circumscribe.

Line stands for the contemplative value in his compositions, and, by the same token, gives unity to the whole; all the rest is—details. That unification of space, within which only one event is represented (Masaccio's strong point) interests him little; his composition co-ordinates figures and objects in a rhythm permeating all the scattered elements.

Though he delights in very delicate colours, his response is more to their beauty than to the play of light on them; indeed he ignores the technique Piero della Francesca transmitted to Pollaiuolo, and remains faithful to the method of handling colour followed by his teacher, Filippo Lippi. He prefers stressing the symbolical value of colours so as to reinforce the expression of his emotion; in short colour is to him a means rather than an end.

It is perhaps significant that Botticelli was a contemporary of Giovanni Bellini. At Florence as at Venice a craving for simple Christian charity was now beginning to be felt, after a phase of high intellectual adventure. In Venice the pursuit of the Christian ideal went more smoothly than in Florence, where it involved spiritual crises, tempests of repentance. It was Giorgione, with his sense of nature's poetry, who followed Giovanni Bellini in Venice. At Florence Michelangelo appreciated Botticelli's line and regarded it as a "monumental" value. True, Michelangelo was very different and brought sweeping changes; none the less one of the sources of his style is to be found in Botticelli.

ANDREA DEL CASTAGNO (1423-1457). CRUCIFIXION (FRAGMENT). FRESCO.
SANT' APOLLONIA MUSEUM, FLORENCE.

ANDREA DEL CASTAGNO

Born in 1423 of a family of shepherds, Andrea del Castagno when still a child went to live in the township of Castagno (whence he acquired his name). At a very early age he showed a quite amazing talent and his devotion to art (" *si spasmiata,*" as Vasari picturesquely describes it) led him to Florence in 1440. There, when only 17, he undertook to paint, to Cosimo de' Medici's order, the likenesses of the traitors vanquished at Anghiari, the battle which established the supremacy of the Medici family at Florence. Young Andrea's work (which has not come down to us) figured on the wall of the Mayoral Palace and depicted the rebels " a little larger than life, " Vasari tells us, " hung by their heels in strange attitudes, very varied and most beautifully rendered." These paintings earned for the artist a great reputation and also the rather sinister nickname "Andrea of the Hanged." It would seem that soon after this he made a stay in Venice where some frescos by him are still to be seen, but in a ruined state. Returning to Florence, he worked in the Cathedral, at the same time as Donatello and Paolo Uccello. He died of plague in 1457, at the early age of 34.

Judging by the account in Vasari's *Lives*, Castagno was a hot-tempered man, unscrupulous and even capable of murder on occasion ; thus he is said to have killed his bosom friend Domenico Veneziano in a fit of jealousy. Actually there are records proving that Veneziano outlived Andrea del Castagno for two years ; so once again Vasari has let his taste for sensationalism get the better of his veracity.

Nevertheless, such is the expressionist violence of his art that we can easily understand how these stories of his ferocity won credence.

Only a small fraction of this artist's output has survived. Apart from some works scattered in collections and museums in Europe and the United States, practically all we have of him is at Florence, chiefly in the S. Apollonia Museum, where a fair number of his frescos have been brought together. Amongst them is a series of figures depicting eminent personages, which once adorned a villa near Florence. We are struck by the strong feeling of violent movement the artist has imparted to these figures, thanks to a method of his own of handling perspective and by the way in which he makes each figure tell out by his vigorous modelling. Different in mood is the large fresco of the *Last Supper*, in which each of the figures is cast, so to speak, in an heroic mould ; this, one of his greatest works, if not psychologically profound, displays great plastic vigour.

The *Crucifixion* here reproduced is also to be seen in this museum. Painted during the last years of the artist's life, it admirably combines two tendencies which elsewhere he often kept apart. Here the expressionist element is mellowed by the beauty of the light, whose limpid serenity tempers the bold, impetuous drawing.

In his inspired moments Andrea del Castagno achieved a happy compromise between his vigorous handling of space and perspective and his feeling for light. While obviously much influenced by Masaccio and by Donatello's sculpture, he went against the general trend of his age in his predilection for portraying violent movement, and in this respect he cuts the figure of a pioneer. Indeed he may be said to have ushered in the dramatic phase of Florentine painting.

ANTONIO POLLAIUOLO

Born in Florence about 1432, Antonio Pollaiuolo stands midway between Castagno and Botticelli, and while in Botticelli's art we feel a passionate regret for a world that is passing away, Pollaiuolo is still full of the optimism of the earlier age, its faith in the future, its zest for new discoveries in every field of knowledge. The freedom of his treatment of his subjects and the power of his drawing make him one of the most remarkable figures of his time.

Little or nothing is known of the man Pollaiuolo was—which is regrettable, for we feel he must have had a very interesting personality. He was a many-sided artist : painter, designer, goldsmith and sculptor all at once, and, whatever branch of art he set his hand to, turned out work of the highest order.

Son of a poulterer (hence the name "Pollaiuolo"), Antonio was the eldest of four brothers, one of whom, Piero, several years his junior, took a hand in almost all his works. We are told that, as a boy, he was apprenticed to a goldsmith ; in his twenties he was evidently still engaged in work of this nature, an order being given him (in conjunction with other artists) for making a silver cross for the altar at St John's.

In 1460, as we learn from one of his letters, he was commissioned by Piero de' Medici to paint, in collaboration with Piero, three large pictures of " The Labours of Hercules." The two small pictures dealing with this theme which used to be in the Uffizi (they disappeared during the recent war) were probably copies made by the artist himself of the larger works. His fondness for the Hercules legend is characteristic ; it gave scope for delineating those movements of the human body under strain or in the exercise of fierce energy in the rendering of which he excelled.

Notable, too, in this connexion, is his predilection for the nude. While the previous generation had been all for "that lovely thing, perspective," Pollaiuolo's contemporaries showed no less enthusiasm for the study of anatomy. For, besides assisting them in the faithful rendering of nature, this knowledge of the human body seemed to them to open up vast possibilities, not only of widening the horizons of figurative art, but also of revealing

POLLAIUOLO (CA. 1432-1498). APOLLO AND DAPHNE. NATIONAL GALLERY, LONDON.

in an effective and poetic manner new aspects of that "discovery of man" which was the pride and the delight of the Renaissance.

Thus amongst the most famous works by this artist is a "Battle of Nudes" (ca. 1470) in which masterful, incisive drawing implements a rhythmic counterpoint of bodies in movement and lances telling out against a background of foliage. We find a similar treatment of nude figures in the fresco at the Villa Gallina, where the theme is a "Dance of Nudes." Though time has played havoc with this fresco, enough remains to show both that exquisiteness of line characteristic of Pollaiuolo and the freedom he permitted himself in rendering forms, while the rhythm of the dance seems almost to merge them into the surrounding air.

For several years after 1460 the only records we have of Pollaiuolo refer solely to his activities as a goldsmith. We learn of his making a tabernacle and candelabra for the Baptistery at St John's and other works of this order. In 1467 he began work on the memorial (in the Church of S. Miniato) of the cardinal representing Portugal at the Holy See. On the wall above the tomb he painted angels raising a curtain, hung like that of a theatre, in front of the niche containing the central picture, in which figure Saints Vincent, Eustace and James, likewise painted by Pollaiuolo. Antonio's brother is known to have taken part in this work but, as usual, it is difficult precisely to determine the share of each. An interesting point is that the use of oils, even for fresco-painting, was now coming in and other artists, including Baldovinetti, were adopting the new technique.

Pollaiuolo was also invited to submit a design for a globe crowning the cupola of Santa Maria del Fiore, on the lines of the design made by Brunelleschi. There was a competition for this work and Verrocchio won it ; the globe was duly installed, but did not survive long, being struck by lightning and shattered in 1492. It would seem that in 1469, on the occasion of a visit he paid to Filippo Lippi at Spoleto, Pollaiuolo went to Rome for the first time, and thus came in contact with the Papal Court. It was now most probably that the two brothers made the figurines "Romulus and Remus and the She-Wolf"— emblem of the Eternal City. Pollaiuolo was again employed by the Papal Court in 1484 when he was commissioned to make the tomb of Pope Sixtus IV at St Peter's. He spent ten years on it, dividing his time between Rome and Florence, and no sooner was it finished than he embarked on a similar task, for the tomb of Pope Innocent VIII, which he completed shortly before his death—indeed the execution betrays some signs of fatigue. In any case his declining years were clouded by misfortune. At Florence he designed the dome of the Santo Spirito Church, intended to outdo in spectacular boldness Brunelleschi's dome, but it collapsed a month after its inauguration. Cruellest blow of all was, undoubtedly, his brother's death, which took place in or about 1496. Another disappointment was the cancellation of a project on which his heart was set : of making, for the Court of Milan, a huge Sforza memorial. Pollaiuolo had looked forward to this work as the crowning achievement of his career, something that would vie with the best of Donatello and Verrocchio, and he submitted several plans, but the Milan Court broke off negotiations with him, so the project came to nothing. Antonio died on February 4, 1498, and was buried beside his brother.

Amongst his most famous works are the large altarpiece in the London National Gallery, *The Martyrdom of St Sebastian*, and, in the same Gallery, the small *Apollo and Daphne*. Here an extreme elegance in rendering movement is allied with a remarkable freedom of execution, and the diffused light swathing the landscape resembles that which Piero della Francesca was the first to introduce. This is a charming work, full of happy ingenuity ; not only is the flying nymph transformed into a tree, but the tree becomes all nature. The *St Sebastian* is a very striking composition. We feel the tension of the bodies of the cross-bowmen grouped round the Saint, while the attitude of the two bowmen in the foreground stooping down in opposing rhythms adds distinction to the arabesque formed by the group of figures as a whole. In the *Rape of Dejanira* in the Jarves Collection (New Haven), it is not only the charm with which the subject is portrayed that compels our admiration, but also the wonderful translucency of the air, due to the ease and fluency of the brushwork ; indeed we have here an anticipation of the art of the great Venetians of the XVIth century.

ANDREA VERROCCHIO

That versatility which we found in Pollaiuolo and which was characteristic of so many artists of the great days of the Renaissance was shared by Verrocchio who was, as Vasari tells us, goldsmith, painter, architect and, above all, sculptor. Many of his works of sculpture have come down to us, but there are only two pictures which can, with absolute certainty, be ascribed to him.

Verrocchio was born in 1436 at Florence and soon established a great reputation for himself as a sculptor. His work in this field was obviously influenced by his early training as a goldsmith and (what is rarer) he also applied in it some of the procedures appropriate to painting. Noteworthy amongst his sculptural works is the bronze *Christ and St Thomas* (the tabernacle is by Donatello) which he made for the Orsanmichele Church at Florence. He began work on this in 1467 and ended it in 1483. In most cases no exact dates can be assigned to Verrocchio's activities. We know, however, that in 1467 the Cathedral Chapter gave him the order for completing the globe which was to crown the dome originally planned by the architect Brunelleschi. In 1472 Verrocchio made the monument of Giovanni and Piero de' Medici in the Sacristy at S. Lorenzo's, a work conspicuous for its harmoniousness and the happily inspired rhythms of its forms ; to the same year may be ascribed his *David*, justly famed for the curious effect of vibrant life the sculptor has imparted to its texture. In 1479 he was commissioned by the Signoria of Venice to make the Colleoni Memorial, on which he started to work in 1481. The majesty of this equestrian statue and the impression it conveys of masterful energy rank it beside that other great equestrian portrait of the Renaissance, Donatello's *Gattamelata*. In 1488 he was in Venice, where he died on October 7. The casting of the statue had not yet taken place ; likewise his monument for the tomb of Cardinal Fonteguerri at Pistoia was completed only after his death.

There is little or no information available regarding Verrocchio's career as a painter. It is a well-established fact that he entrusted a large share of the execution of his paintings to his assistants, amongst whom were Leonardo, Perugino, Ghirlandaio, Credi and probably Botticelli—to name only the outstanding figures. We know that several of the works described as being the master's were entirely painted by his pupils ; as, for example, the altarpiece in the Pistoia Cathedral, which is obviously by the hand of Lorenzo di Credi. Two works unquestionably his are the *Madonna* at Berlin and the *Baptism* at the Uffizi. But in the latter work Leonardo's collaboration, first mentioned by Vasari, is now regarded as indubitable. In this picture, painted in or about 1470, we are conscious of the simultaneous presence of two tendencies, that of the art of the XVth-century in its death-throes and that of the new art sponsored by the Cinquecento. But though, in theory, it should be easy enough to distinguish between the work done by the master and that of his young pupil, in practice it is impossible to draw a hard-and-fast line between their respective shares. However it is generally accepted that Leonardo was responsible for one of the two angels (the first on the left) and also for the landscape background.

Verrocchio belongs to the same world as Pollaiuolo and their temperaments had much in common ; though their methods were different, both felt the same desire for an ever greater mastery of the *matière* of art. But whereas in the work of Pollaiuolo there is always a touch of spontaneous poetic fantasy, Verrocchio's displays (as Vasari noted) a certain harshness, which however is not lacking in strength and dignity. There is no lyricism in Verrocchio ; rather, we find a habit of ponderation leading him to concentrate on statuesque postures indicated by naturalistic, incisive drawing. His power as an artist derives from technical proficiency and conscientious execution. In fact no one could have been better qualified for the early training of a genius so venturesome as Leonardo's.

Though he shared his activities between painting and sculpture, most of his output was in the latter field. Verrochio's feeling for plastic values was happily allied with superb craftsmanship, indeed the mantle of Donatello had fallen on his shoulders. Thus he became

VERROCCHIO (1436-1488). BAPTISM OF CHRIST. UFFIZI, FLORENCE.

the leading figure of XVth-century Florence, and his studio the most famous and sought-after of all.   Thanks to the feeling of life that he imparts to it Verrocchio's sculpture stands out amongst the work of his contemporaries, though he obviously underwent the influences of other great artists.   The presence of such influences was natural enough, considering the conditions of Florentine art in his time — the close contacts between the artists living there and the officially organized competitions that were the order of the day.

SANDRO BOTTICELLI

Idolized by his contemporaries, forgotten after his death, Botticelli was " discovered " in the XIXth century in England by the Pre-Raphaelite painter Dante Gabriel Rossetti, by Swinburne, Walter Pater and Ruskin. Surprising as it is that a painter of such conspicuous genius should have undergone so long an eclipse, what is even more surprising is that his discoverers for the most part saw in him no more than an engaging " Primitive, " with a wistful, somewhat decadent charm. Yet, while it may be granted that there is more than a touch of nostalgia in Botticelli's exquisitely refined art, he shows no lack of manly vigour when his feelings are engaged.

Botticelli realized that the old order was passing for ever and the knowledge saddened him ; but his regret was for more than the loss of a familiar climate, it was bound up with his deep religious faith. For the Church as she then was and her institutions no longer satisfied him and when, following the preachings of Savonarola, a gust of reform swept Florence, he made no secret of his discomposure, even though any idea of playing an active part in the movement was ruled out by his fastidious temperament. Masaccio's Adam and Eve took their sad way from the lost Paradise " with wandering steps and slow, " but at least they knew that one day they would regain it ; Botticelli's exiles know that they are banished from it for ever. Some smile forlornly, others fix their gaze on a supernal world, but all alike have lost the proud self-confidence, the heaven-scaling hopes of the Men of the Renaissance. With the death of Lorenzo the Magnificent in 1492 Florence had abruptly lost her power and prestige, and in Botticelli's day not only were men losing their confidence in Man, but the links between their religious faith and the Church were wearing thin. Savonarola's homilies, *De ruina mundi* and *De ruina Ecclesiae*, were sadly apposite.

Sandro di Filipepi, known as Botticelli (the surname given an elder brother), was born at Florence in 1444 or the beginning of 1445. His father, a tanner, was one of the many artisans in a small way dwelling near the Ognissanti Church. Sandro was the youngest of seven children. When still a boy he entered Filippo Lippi's *bottega* (before this, it seems, he had been working for a goldsmith), probably at the time when Filippo Lippi was employed at the Prato Cathedral. No traces of young Sandro's handiwork are discernable in the output of his master's " workshop " during this period, but the influence of Filippo Lippi persisted in his art over a long period.

The earliest work known positively to be his is the *Fortezza* (Fortitude) one of the " Virtues " originally allotted to Piero Pollaiuolo in the competition for the murals at the Mercanzia Tribunal. It was probably the Medici who insisted on his being given this figure to paint, despite protests from the Guild of Painters. For Botticelli was not yet a member of the Guild, and joined it only a good deal later, though in 1472 he set up his own *bottega*, in which Filippino Lippi, son of his teacher, was one of his assistants. About the same time there was a proposal to employ him on the decoration of the Campo Santo at Pisa, but the sample of his work that he submitted at Florence was judged unsatisfactory and Benozzo Gozzoli finished the work alone.

Nevertheless Botticelli was not only highly thought of at the time but he enjoyed the active patronage of Lorenzo de' Medici who, himself a poet and connoisseur, loved to gather round him at his Court all the most enlightened spirits of the age.

Botticelli must have had a happy youth, spent in the company of such men as Verrocchio, Pollaiuolo (whom he certainly met at the Medici Court) and Leonardo, who like himself was a member of the " Company of St Luke. "

In 1475 Lorenzo de' Medici had him make the banner for the great tournament given in honour of his brother Giuliano ; the banner has disappeared, but a description of it survives in the verses of his contemporary Poliziano. It was during this period that Botticelli painted those two works on mythological themes, *Primavera* and *The Birth of Venus*, which rank to-day amongst the best known works of all Italian art. The Pre-Raphaelites read all sorts of symbols into the former work and indeed one of the charms of *Primavera* is the evocative richness of its imagery. Nevertheless it is known that the artist had the theme imposed on him—it was not of his own choosing—and the first to name the picture *Primavera* was Vasari. Moreover we gather from contemporary writings that the real subject of the picture was Venus and her retinue. Be this as it may, Botticelli has exquisitely rendered here that feeling of sadness which attends the sight of youthful grace, so fragile and so ephemeral; of " Beauty that must die "—a feeling which ever haunted the minds of the Florentines of the epoch, and was expressed in Lorenzo de' Medici's lines :

" Be joyful while ye may,
" And count not on the morrow... "

Here Botticelli has achieved a union so complete between the visionary imagination and perfection of form that this picture has come to be regarded as the supreme expression of the culture of its day. Yet we may perhaps regret that this aspect of Botticelli's art has been so much insisted on at the expense of the others.

In 1478 the conspiracy of the Pazzi caused an upheaval at Florence, Giuliano being murdered by the conspirators and Lorenzo escaping a like fate only by a hair's breadth. After the revolt had been put down Lorenzo consolidated his power and wreaked fierce vengeance on his enemies. He asked Botticelli, now his Court Painter, to paint the eight traitors hung by their necks or feet on the gateway of the Dogana, this fresco being a complement to that made by Andrea del Castagno for Cosimo. Both frescos were destroyed in 1494 when the Medici were driven out of Florence.

The *St Augustine* fresco (dated 1480) in the Ognissanti Church enables us to understand why a contemporary described Botticelli's art as " virile, " for the compelling power of this work is undeniable. In a bright sheen of colours the figure of the Saint is given its full plastic value, and in his gaze we feel a presentiment of the destiny awaiting him. Botticelli's art is extraordinarily complex ; for all its amazing virtuosity, he makes us feel that he is always chary of pressing this too far and lapsing into rhetorical effects ; indeed it is this restraint he imposes on his art that constitutes its strength. Likewise, though none has surpassed him in sensuous grace and the art of expressing emotions whether tender or keyed-up to their highest pitch, he circumscribes them, even at their intensest, with a clean-cut and incisive, if profoundly vibrant, line. This *St Augustine* is probably the most powerful of his works during the period preceding the death of Lorenzo de' Medici.

Botticelli's activity was prodigious during the twelve years from 1480 to 1492. No sooner did the strained relations between the Papacy and Florence come to an end than Pope Sixtus IV summoned several Florentine painters to Rome and set them to decorating the Chapel which subsequently was named after him the " Sistine, " along with Perugino and Signorelli. Thus Domenico Ghirlandaio, Cosimo Rosselli and Botticelli were in Rome together in 1481. A contract (the only one) relating to the Sistine Chapel that has come down to us shows that in October of that year each of the Florentines and Perugino had already finished a fresco, and that they were starting on ten others. When these were completed is not known, but by 1482 Botticelli was back in Florence. After this stay in Rome his reputation stood higher than ever and he was given a number of orders, some of them for decorating *palazzi* and churches ; on all these paintings he had others working with him.

The two " Tornabuoni " frescos at the Louvre formed part of the murals he painted at the Medici Palace at Volterra, the Villa Tornabuoni-Careggi. Besides a number of small works on religious subjects he was commissioned to make several large altarpieces. His output was in fact both vast and varied at this time. Amongst his most famous works of this period are the drawings for Dante's *Divine Comedy*. These were commissioned by Lorenzo de Pierfrancesco de' Medici (Lorenzo's cousin); Botticelli seems to have begun work on them before he went to Rome, but he completed the series only in 1503.

In 1491 the Committee of the " Arte della Lana " held a meeting under the patronage of Lorenzo to make arrangements for the decoration in mosaic of St Zenobius' Chapel in the

SANDRO BOTTICELLI (1444 OR 1445-1510).   THE THREE GRACES.   DETAIL FROM "PRIMAVERA".   UFFIZI, FLORENCE.

Cathedral.   Several artists, Botticelli amongst them, were engaged, but the project came to nothing.   The next year was a disastrous one for Florence ; Lorenzo died and the political stability which had made good the power of Florence under Lorenzo's rule ended with his death.   Though Botticelli suffered no immediate loss, he may well have felt great anxiety about the future, and it was now began those accesses of despair and melancholia which cast their shadows on the last phase of his art.

SANDRO BOTTICELLI (1444 OR 1445-1510).   LA DERELITTA.   PALLAVICINI COLLECTION, ROME.

SANDRO BOTTICELLI (1444 OR 1445-1510). ST JOHN. DETAIL FROM THE MADONNA OF SAN BARNABA. UFFIZI, FLORENCE.

SANDRO BOTTICELLI (1444 OR 1445-1510). ST AUGUSTINE. OGNISSANTI, FLORENCE

SANDRO BOTTICELLI (1444 OR 1445-1510). MIRACLES OF ST ZENOBIUS.
NATIONAL GALLERY, LONDON.

For some ten years the Dominican Girolamo Savonarola had been spreading dismay amongst pious Catholics by his terrifying prophecies and his fierce denunciations of the worldliness of the age. And when presently one disaster followed another in Italy, his influence increased by rapid strides. Naturally he met with vigorous opposition, and finally he was forbidden to preach and, refusing to obey, was excommunicated, imprisoned, tortured and hanged, on May 23, 1498. His body and those of two other Dominican Brothers were burnt in the presence of the populace. The tragic end of Savonarola, coupled with the fact that his prophecies were being so visibly fulfilled in the catastrophic period on which Italy had entered, and in the iniquities of those in high places, made a deep impression on Botticelli, and, though he had never actually been one of Savonarola's followers, he fretted himself into a state of great depression. It is recorded that in 1499 he asked one of Savonarola's judges what the charges against him really were, and was given the answer : " Sandro, would you have me tell you the truth ? Then know that we found in him no mortal or even venial sin. But if we had not had him and his zealots put to death, the populace would surely have sacked our homes and torn us limb from limb. " The injustice of this attitude and his daily intercourse with his brother, who was a fanatical disciple of Savonarola, added to his despondency. At the same time his religious feeling, always deep, developed an almost morbid intensity, and the suavity with which he treated religious themes in his early work now gave place more and more to an extreme emotionalism of line, colour and composition.

In the *Nativity* (National Gallery, London) the Madonna and Child are surrounded by distraught human figures, vainly yearning for the tranquil bliss of the angelic host. Thus, too, in the altarpieces portraying incidents in the life of St Zenobius, Botticelli gives the action architectural settings whose pure lines and serenity emphasize the emotive tension of the rest of the picture. He discards much that his age deemed essential, such as geometrical unity and differing relations between figures in terms of nearness or remoteness ; his one concern is for the rendering of emotion in his line. It wavers, breaks off and flows again in rhythms throbbing with wild regret, the anguish of mortality confronting death. This is indeed a far cry from the glad vision of Venus rising blithely from the waves, or even the serene beauty of his Madonnas bending above the Child. The total sincerity of Botticelli's art where his deeper feelings are involved makes him one of the most appealing figures of the XVth century, which spiritually, if not literally, ended with him.

TOWARDS THE
HIGH RENAISSANCE

LUCA SIGNORELLI (?1450-1523).   THE HOLY FAMILY.   UFFIZI, FLORENCE.

More still than Botticelli, Luca Signorelli may be regarded as a precursor of Michelangelo, and not only on the strength of his "Last Judgement" at Orvieto Cathedral. His "tondo" at the Uffizi admirably illustrates the heroic grandeur of his style; wholly immune from wistfulness or tender imaginings, it has that terrific driving force known in Italy as "terribilità," a force deriving not only from the expressive power of the rendering but from the difficult problems of craftsmanship that exponents of this "terribilità" went out of their way to tackle.

Signorelli's style is exceptionally rich, including as it does both Pollaiuolo's line and Piero della Francesca's light. Moreover Signorelli was the first of the Tuscans systematically to employ the fine shades of Flemish colour. Hence his rejection of bright hues—pointing the way to the art of Leonardo.

Between Botticelli (and Signorelli) and Michelangelo, as between Bellini and Giorgione, a miracle intervened which once again changed the whole aspect of painting. And that miracle was—Leonardo da Vinci.

In 1480 Leonardo began his "Adoration of the Magi" (now in the Uffizi); though the work of a young man of twenty-eight, it displays a style that has completely found itself. It is an unfinished work; giving the finishing touches irked Leonardo. At that time he painted as he drew, at a great rate, in the grip of a creative frenzy. It was only later in life, and with an effort, that he schooled himself to the slow, painstaking craftsmanship preconized by Florentine tradition. In this tendency towards a "judicious unfinish" as it has been called, we see an essentially modern spirit of independence: the pride of the creative artist defying the mere craftsman.

And now the surfaces patterned with bright colours dear to traditional art vanished abruptly. The whole picture seemed drowned in flooding darkness, whence emerged restless phantoms, lacking in plastic substance but imbued with a unique intensity of expression. It is no hyperbole to say that Leonardo painted souls rather than bodies.

A smouldering unrest pervades alike worshippers and worshipped, even those who are distant from the central action. Thus at one swoop, and at the very time *when Botticelli was nostalgically seeking a return to the past, Leonardo swept aside all that had passed for colour and drawing hitherto—for the greater glory of the human soul. His drawing is rapid, intermittent, sometimes striking at the very heart of the form portrayed, sometimes outlining it from afar. His chiaroscuro stresses dark passages rather than highlights and suggests muted colours in the shadows. Everywhere he sacrifices colour; fine shades, his "sfumato," replace it. Thus he can give free play to movement, which he renders without the help of contour-lines, by an all-pervading vibration, which is as it were a manner of painting and drawing simultaneously.*

Artists preceding Leonardo had made a fetish of perspective and anatomy. As a scientist he studied these with due attention, but his universal genius ranged much farther, covering all fields of knowledge and research. Yet we feel that he discarded these purely scientific interests once he took up his brush and set his fancies free to rove in an enchanted dusk where the day is dying and the night has yet to fall.

With Leonardo modern art and modern life were knocking at the door. That XVth-century culture which with its confidence in Man, its moral energy, and its daring intellectualism, had given the world so many masterpieces, was drawing to an end. And that end was the beginning of the disasters which, as well as glories, the following century was to bring to Italy.

LEONARDO DA VINCI (1452-1519). MADONNA AND CHILD. DETAIL FROM THE ADORATION OF THE MAGI.
UFFIZI, FLORENCE.

Printed in Switzerland